Artisan Cheese

OF THE PACIFIC NORTHWEST

Artisan Cheese
OF THE PACIFIC NORTHWEST

Tami Parr

THE COUNTRYMAN PRESS
WOODSTOCK, VERMONT

ISBN 978-0-88150-834-5

Interior photos by the author unless otherwise noted
Book design and composition by Eugenie S. Delaney
Maps by Paul Woodward, © The Countryman Press
Published by The Countryman Press, P.O. Box 748, Woodstock, Vermont 05091

Distributed by W. W. Norton & Company, Inc., 500 Fifth Avenue, New York, NY 10110

Printed in the United States of America

10 9 8 7 6 5 4 3 2 1

ACKNOWLEDGMENTS

Five years ago, I started a blog called the Pacific Northwest Cheese Project. At the time, I intended for the site to be a creative outlet and a way to explore locally made artisan cheese. I'm thankful for everyone who has visited my Web site and I'm thrilled to be able to further the conversation about local artisan cheese-making by writing this book.

I owe tremendous thanks to every cheesemaker in this book for their willingness to talk about their lives and work, and for welcoming me onto their farms and into their homes. Thanks to editors Martha Holmberg of *The Oregonian* and Angie Jabine, formerly of *Northwest Palate,* for their enthusiasm about local artisan cheese and their willingness to publish an unknown writer. Thanks also to everyone at Countryman Press for all of their patience and hard work in putting this book together.

Others provided encouragement, editing, and cheese along the way: Steve Jones, David Gremmels, Diane Morgan, Lisbeth Goddik, Marc Bates, Jack Joyce, Luan Schooler, Sasha Davies, and Kurt Dammeier. Thanks also to Laura Byrne Russell for her recipe expertise, Leigh Salmon for her gorgeous cover photo, and to my partner, Anna—without her support and encouragement none of this would have been possible.

CONTENTS

ix

Washington
and
British Columbia

British Columbia Cheesemakers

1. Farm House Natural Cheeses
2. Goat's Pride Dairy
3. Ridgecrest Dairy
4. Scardillo Cheese Co.
5. Hilary's Artisan Cheese Co.
6. Little Qualicum Cheeseworks
7. Moonstruck Organic Cheeses
8. Natural Pastures Cheese Co.
9. Salt Spring Island Cheese
10. Fairburn Farm
11. Carmelis Goat Cheese
12. D Dutchmen Dairy
13. Gort's Gouda
14. Happy Days Goat Dairy
15. Jerseyland Organics

Continues...

16. Mountain Meadow Sheep Dairy
17. Poplar Grove Cheese Co.
18. Triple Island Farm
19. The Village Cheese Co.
20. Kootenay Alpine Cheese Co.

Washington Cheesemakers

1. Beecher's Handmade Cheeses
2. Estrella Family Creamery
3. Mt. Townsend Creamery
4. Port Madison Farms
5. Quail Croft Goat Cheese
6. River Valley Ranch
7. Sea Breeze Farm
8. Steamboat Island Goat Farm
9. Black Sheep Creamery
10. Blue Rose Dairy
11. Twin Oaks Creaery
12. Dee Creek Farm
13. Rosecrest Farm
14. Willapa Hils Farmstead Cheese
15. Apple Farms
16. El Michoacano
17. Golden Glen Creamery
18. Gothberg Farms
19. Grace Harbor Farms
20. Pleasant Valley Dairy
21. Samish Bay Cheese Co.
22. Silver Springs Creamery
23. Alpine Lakes Sheep Cheese
24. Larkhaven Farm

25. Monteillet Fromagerie
26. Pine Stump Farm
27. Queseria Bendita
28. Quillisascut Cheese Co.
29. Sally Jackson Cheeses
30. W.S.U. Creamery
31. Sunny Pine Farm

Kamloops
Merritt
Kelowna
Courtenay
Vancouver
Bellingham
Victoria
Port Angeles
Everett
Seattle
Tacoma
Olympia
Ellensburg
Aberdeen
Astoria
Longview
Potrland

British Columbia
Washington
CANADA
U.S.
Washington
Idaho
Spokane

Mt. Baker
Mt. Rainier
Mt. St. Helens
Mt. Hood

Strait of Juan de Fuca

PACIFIC OCEAN

Washington
Oregon

N

0   Statute Miles   50

Paul Woodward, © The Countryman Press

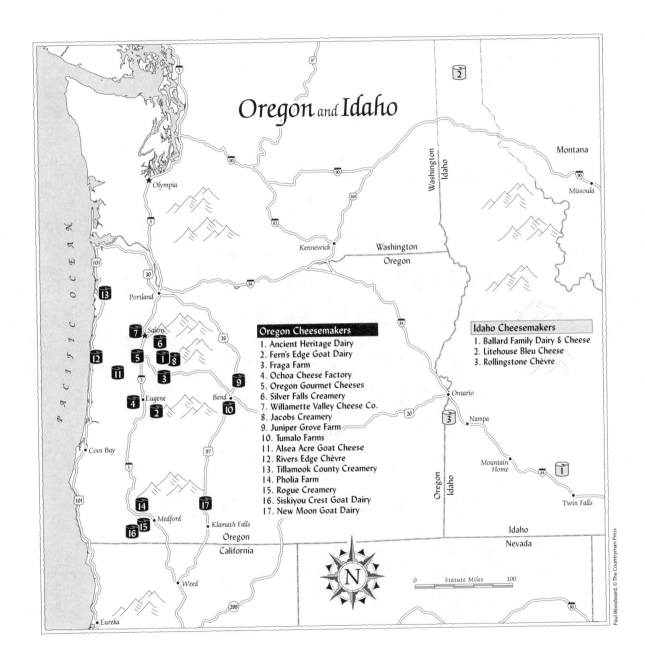

Oregon and Idaho

Oregon Cheesemakers
1. Ancient Heritage Dairy
2. Fern's Edge Goat Dairy
3. Fraga Farm
4. Ochoa Cheese Factory
5. Oregon Gourmet Cheeses
6. Silver Falls Creamery
7. Willamette Valley Cheese Co.
8. Jacobs Creamery
9. Juniper Grove Farm
10. Tumalo Farms
11. Alsea Acre Goat Cheese
12. Rivers Edge Chèvre
13. Tillamook County Creamery
14. Pholia Farm
15. Rogue Creamery
16. Siskiyou Crest Goat Dairy
17. New Moon Goat Dairy

Idaho Cheesemakers
1. Ballard Family Dairy & Cheese
2. Litehouse Bleu Cheese
3. Rollingstone Chèvre

Statute Miles

N

Paul Woodward, © The Countryman Press

INTRODUCTION

*I*magine the following scenario: three regional festivals, with a combined attendance in excess of 100,000 people. Each festival celebrates a product made locally, a product that most everyone enjoys. Producers of this product have multiplied rapidly over the past decade, and experts estimate conservatively that hundreds of distinct varieties of the product are currently available to consumers both locally and nationally.

What I'm talking about is the emerging artisan cheese renaissance in the Pacific Northwest. Several years ago, no one would have thought cheese a worthy subject for any kind of festival. Today Oregon, Washington, and British Columbia all hold annual festivals celebrating artisan cheese (not to mention a new festival now being held in Northern California). Fewer than 25 artisan cheesemakers were making cheese in the Pacific Northwest in 2000, and their products were not widely available to consumers in markets or restaurants. In 2008 that number has almost tripled, currently standing at 70 and growing. More than 30 new cheesemakers have started up since 2005. If we assume that each artisan operating today produces three types of cheese—a conservative estimate, considering that many make a dozen or more—that adds up to well over 200 different types of locally made artisan cheese available today. This is what they're celebrating at the Seattle Cheese Festival in Seattle, Washington, the Oregon Cheese Festival in Central Point, Oregon, and the Granville Island Cheese Festival in Vancouver, British Columbia.

WHILE WE ARE CERTAINLY in the midst of a cheesemaking renaissance, artisan cheesemaking is by no means a new phenomenon. Immigrants brought Old World traditions to the New World from Europe, and homesteading pioneers traveling to the West made cheese just as they made all of their food. Cheesemaking (artisan or otherwise) was once a part of everyday life. Because milk is such a perishable product, dairy, milk, and butter production was once completely local—dairy farmers pooled their milk at a central location, usually

Ah, for the life of Tilly of Tillamook*

*Tillamook County, Oregon

Life is just a bed of buttercups for Tilly. All day long she relaxes in the green pastures of Tillamook County — eating succulent, moist grasses — drinking cool, crystal-clear spring water and meditatively chewing her cud. Then in the night she sleeps in clean, fresh straw and dreams of tomorrow in Tillamook. Talk about the life of Reilly! What about the life of Tilly?

No wonder Tilly's milk results in America's prize-winning, best-tasting cheddar cheese — Tillamook. Though, of course, the cheese-making folks at Tillamook have something to do with it too! They brought their recipe for making natural cheddar cheese from the old country — generations ago. Tillamook cheddar is made of rich, pure milk and then allowed to age slowly and naturally to just the right degree of tasty perfection — sharp or mild, but full-flavored.

Look for Tillamook in wedges, slices, loaves at your nearest grocer.

Store-cut wedges
Mild or Sharp

Sharp over one year old   Mild but full flavored

Tillamook Cheese
natural, aged cheddar ... never processed

Early Tillamook ads, like this one featuring Tilly, highlighted Northwest regional elements like climate and terroir

within the same county, where it was bottled and distributed. Many local cooperatives also made cheese. With the advent of the interstate highway and refrigeration, dairy gradually lost its local character. Northwest dairy giants such as Tillamook and Darigold evolved from these humble origins. Eventually centralized, industrial-scale factories took over most dairy and cheese production.

So what has changed to create a rebirth in small-scale farmstead and artisan cheesemaking? Small producers began to emerge in significant numbers in the 1970s as postwar baby boomers first began to turn toward organic and wholesome food alternatives. The Pacific Northwest was part of this trend; cheesemakers George Train of Pleasant Valley Dairy in Northwest Washington and Sally Jackson in Eastern Washington both began making and selling cheese in the 1970s. One of the most important factors in the dramatic resurgence in cheesemaking during the past decade is consumers' growing interest in local and sustainable food. Whether attributable to environmental concerns or to a search for wholesome food choices, consumer interest in all facets of sustainability has driven them toward local producers of all types, including artisan cheesemakers. And where demand exists, producers multiply to meet it.

Closely related is the rise of regional farmers' markets during the same period. The Oregon Farmers' Markets Association estimates that 90,000 people attend a farmers' market in the state on any given weekend. The Washington State Farmers' Markets Association puts the number at 200,000, and that's not including Seattle's Pike Place Market, which receives more than 10 million visitors a year. Where in the past artisan cheesemakers such as Pierre Kolisch of Juniper Grove Farm and Chuck and Karen Evans of Rollingstone Chèvre made the rounds of restaurants and retail markets in urban areas to distribute their products, today's artisans can sell products at farmers' markets and eager consumers come to them. Farmers' markets have, in turn, made handmade artisan cheese accessible to more people.

Economic factors play a role as well. The Pacific Northwest has of late enjoyed economic prosperity relative to the rest of the country, as evidenced by the dramatic population growth coupled with rapidly rising property values. More and more people in our area have the disposable income to be able to enjoy a wider range of foods than they would have several decades ago. These same people are traveling abroad and, upon returning home, seeking out quality local wines and cheeses like those they experienced in Europe. The rise of Northwest wine industry and the microbrew revolution have also contributed significantly to the public's food education and focused all of us on seeking quality food and beverages across the spectrum.

ANY MENTION OF THE PACIFIC NORTHWEST conjures up archetypal images like salmon, Douglas Fir trees, and bald eagles. Cheese doesn't come to mind as a product typically associated with the region as it is in places like Quebec, Wisconsin, or Vermont. Still, you might be surprised to know that Idaho is the third largest cheese producing state in the United States, behind perennial leaders Wisconsin and California. This region is, in fact, a significant presence in the cheese industry. Industrial production goes hand in hand with a significant presence of dairy farms, and it is from dairy farms that many small artisan cheesemakers spring forth.

The Northwest is unique in artisan cheesemaking for a number of reasons, not the least of which is its diverse terroir. We have artisans making cheese in coastal marine climates, like Pat Morford of Rivers Edge Chèvre near the Oregon Coast, or Kelli Estrella of Estrella

Family Creamery in Montesano, Washington, just inland from the Washington Coast. Cheese-makers populate fertile agricultural valleys such as the Willamette Valley in Oregon, the Skagit Valley in Washington, and the Fraser Valley in British Columbia. We have artisan cheese-makers located in the high desserts of Central Oregon as well as the Okanagan Valley of East-ern British Columbia. Each distinct microclimate brings its effects to bear on the products coming out of the region. In short, in the Pacific Northwest, the terroir is endless.

In addition, the Northwest's relatively mild climate translates into a long growing sea-son, which means extra months of green grass for dairy animals to graze on. West of the Cascade Mountain Range, which stretches from Northern California, through Oregon and Washington, then on to British Columbia, animals are able to graze on pasture for as many as 10 months out of the year or more. Green grass delivers distinct components in milk, trans-lating into cheesemaking nectar, which brings flavor and complexity to the finished product.

An additional note on regionalism: I've deliberately chosen to cross political boundaries and include British Columbia in this book along with artisan cheesemakers of the Northwest-ern United States. I think British Columbia belongs in this book for a number of reasons, not the least of which is that this Canadian province is home to many exceptional artisan cheese-makers. However, if you want to enjoy cheese from across the border in either direction, you will have to travel to secure your desired cheese, or otherwise be lost in a complex vortex of import/export regulations. Despite this practical reality, cheesemakers regionwide face simi-lar hurdles in developing and maintaining their farms and operations and have much in com-mon, including economic pressures, marketing issues, and climate concerns. I cling to the hope that someday Americans and Canadians will all be able to enjoy each other's cheese with impunity.

The future looks bright for cheesemaking in the Pacific Northwest. As the industry continues to grow, change is inevitable. Time will no doubt bring an increase in the quality and variety of cheeses available. More cheesemakers will experiment with sheep's milk, a relatively rare commodity in this region, but exceptionally good for making cheese. More specialized products like mixed-milk cheeses are still relatively uncommon in the Pacific Northwest, as are washed-rind cheeses. Hispanic-style and East Indian—style ethnic cheeses (underappreciated as handmade cheese specialties) will likely be an area of future growth.

Make no mistake about it, the next decade will bring changes in the world of artisan cheesemaking. While all indications are that the artisan cheese renaissance will continue at least for the foreseeable future, it's important to remember that artisan cheesemaking is an expensive craft. Many small cheesemakers suffer the same pressures as farmers in other industries, operating on small profit margins with high overhead and increasing costs. A bad sales year or a down economy can quickly put them out of business. You will read many stories in this book about farmers who turned to artisan cheesemaking as a means of preserving their farms and their way of life; they are literally banking on the rising tide of interest in artisan cheese to survive. Consumers have, for now, responded enthusiastically to artisan cheese, but when budgets are tight artisan cheese may be perceived as expendable despite its virtues as a wholesome, locally made product.

Change is inevitable simply because some of the Northwest's best and most established cheesemakers have been around for decades. In British Columbia, Arie Gort, the first small artisan cheesemaker in that region, recently retired and sold his farm and cheesemaking business. George Train, founder of Pleasant Valley Dairy, has passed his cheesemaking operation on to daughter Joyce and her family. Several other cheese operations in British Columbia have changed hands over the past several years, including McLennan Creek Goat Dairy (now Goat's Pride Dairy at McLennan Creek) and Mountain Meadow Sheep Dairy. Other cheesemakers are quietly looking for buyers or exploring alternatives, including closing their operations completely. Early industry trailblazers will not be around forever, and some of the cheeses we cherish today will inevitably be lost in the future.

NO MATTER WHERE YOU LIVE in the Northwest, you are certain to be able to find a handmade cheese produced nearby. Whether that cheese is made from cow, goat, or sheep's milk, whether fresh or aged, whether it tastes mild or tangy, Northwest artisan-made cheeses are of a quality comparable to any artisan cheese in the nation.

The local artisan cheesemakers you will read about in this book are hardworking folks committed to their craft. Cheese is a labor-intensive product that many cheesemakers describe as more of a way of life than a job. Your local artisan juggles a variety of duties, including farm and animal management, maintaining sanitary facilities, packaging products, as well as sales, distribution, and marketing. It's a wonder that cheesemakers have time to sleep, much less make cheese. Yet despite the odds and hardships, making cheese is a labor of love for most producers and they continue to do it because of an abiding love for the art and craft of making a wholesome, healthy product. The results of Northwest cheesemakers' efforts are award-winning, nationally recognized products that are in great demand locally and nationally. We are truly privileged to enjoy the fruits of their labor.

Never has there been a better time to taste, try, and enjoy local artisan cheeses. I hope this book will be a useful guide to your cheese explorations.

CHAPTER 1

OREGON

Willamette Valley

Central Oregon • *Oregon Coast*

Southern Oregon

WILLAMETTE VALLEY

1. ANCIENT HERITAGE DAIRY

KATHY AND PAUL OBRINGER

42067 Hwy. 226

Scio, OR 97374

503-394-2649

ancientheritagedairy.com

SHEEP AND COW'S MILK

STYLES OF CHEESE

Fresh

Scio Feta

Soft-Ripened

Adelle *(sheep and cow's milk blend)*

Valentine

Aged

Hannah Bridge Heritage *(sheep and cow's milk blend)*

Rosa

Scio Heritage

Washed-Rind

Opal Creek

Ancient Heritage Dairy became Oregon's only sheep's milk cheesemaker when they opened in 2006

Kathy Obringer still remembers the salty Greek sheep's milk feta she sold while working at Mecklenburg's in Cincinnati, Ohio. As a sculptor and painter, she probably would have been surprised at the time to know, that decades later, she'd be making that same cheese herself.

The catalyst that triggered this new creative endeavor came when Kathy and her husband, Paul, were living in Portland, Oregon, and two of their children developed allergies. The family moved to a farm and began to explore the possibility of farming full time. Kathy says, "We moved out where there was no chemical spraying and good air for the kids to breathe, but we found out how much we loved dairying."

The Obringers have since built a thriving family business raising sheep and cows and making cheese on 80 acres in Scio, Oregon (about an hour southeast of Portland). Kathy doesn't have much time for art anymore, though she did paint the watercolor art that appears on Ancient Heritage's labels. Now her creative energies are all directed toward making the delectable soft-ripened and aged cheeses that have turned heads all over Oregon. "Our biggest wish is to connect people to a source of deep nourishment through the food they eat," she says.

Hannah Bridge Heritage is rubbed with olive oil and cocoa during the aging process

2. FERN'S EDGE GOAT DAIRY

39456 Hwy. 58

Lowell, OR 97452

541-937-3506

fernsedgedairy.com

GOAT'S MILK

The goats at Fern's Edge graze on a wooded hillside overlooking Dexter Lake near Eugene

STYLES OF CHEESE

Fresh

Fresh chèvre, plain and flavored

Soft-Ripened

Zion Peak Pyramid Camembert

The goats that give their milk for Fern's Edge cheeses are famous—they're part of the nationally recognized Mt. Zion Alpine goat herd, whose bloodlines have been developed through decades of careful breeding by Shari Reyna. Over time, the Reynas came to realize that goat breeding wasn't as profitable as it had been in the past, so they turned to cheese-making as a means of sustaining the farm long-term.

After several years spent constructing the milking and cheesemaking facility, Fern's Edge Goat Dairy started operation in 2006. They started out making fresh chévres, both plain and flavored with pesto, dried chanterelles (picked locally), and dill. Their fresh pesto chévre was an award winner at the American Dairy Goat Association competition in 2007. Currently, the Reynas are developing a line of soft-ripened cheeses and hope to expand their line to include goat's milk yogurt and butter in the future.

Mt. Chanterelle, a pyramid of fresh chévre coated with dried, locally picked chanterelle mushrooms

3. FRAGA FARM

JAN AND LARRY NIELSEN
28580 Pleasant Valley Rd.
Sweet Home, OR 97386
541-367-3891
fragafarm.com
GOAT'S MILK, CERTIFIED ORGANIC

VISITORS
By appointment

Fraga Farm is named after Jan Nielson's grandmother, Agnes Fraga

STYLES OF CHEESE

Fresh
> **Feta**
> **Fresh Chèvre, plain and flavored**
> **Goatzarella** *(goat's milk mozzarella)*

Aged
> **Farm House, plain and flavored**
> **Raw–Milk Cheddar**
> **Rio Santiam**

Jan Nielsen forged her love of the farming life while visiting grandmother Agnes Fraga's 120-acre farm in Castro Valley, California, near San Francisco. Later, after working and living in the Bay Area for 20 years, Jan and her husband, Larry, decided to make a transition. They moved to Sweet Home, Oregon, and started the new incarnation of Fraga Farm.

What started out as a retirement project developed into today's full-time, thriving cheese-making operation. "I knew I wanted to have goats, but I never thought of making cheese," says Jan. She learned the ropes experimenting with making ice cream, yogurt, and the like. Meanwhile, Larry constructed the goat barn, pens, and the cheese room. Crafting cheese that was consistently edible took time and experimentation— "a lot of the cheese went to the chickens at first," Jan says, "but once we learned about different cultures and techniques, it became

Jan and Larry Nielsen make Oregon's only certified organic goat cheese

cheese we could eat!" One early success came when their neighbor, Jim, gave them a recipe for a farmhouse cheese that his mother had made—it tasted good and their friends loved it, too. Fraga Farm became licensed to make and sell cheese in 2000.

Fraga Farm bears the distinction of being Oregon's only certified organic goat dairy. "It goes back to my grandmother," says Jan. "She was the first person I knew who recycled before anyone else did. She used natural remedies for everything, like repelling ants by putting lemon juice in the corners of the house. So it came naturally to me not to want to use chemicals and to nurture healthy animals." Jan puts her grandmother's principles to work every day making wholesome organic goat's milk cheeses.

4. OCHOA CHEESE FACTORY

9496 Airport Rd., #11 & 12
Eugene, OR 97402
541-228-7327

COW'S MILK

STYLES OF CHEESE

Fresh
Queso Fresco

Francisco Ochoa and his family have been making Queso Fresco in Eugene since 2003. Using a family recipe, they produce about 2,000 pounds of cheese a week that is distributed to Hispanic markets across Oregon and Washington.

5. Oregon Gourmet Cheeses

BRIAN RICHTER, CHEESEMAKER

815 1st Ave. E

Albany, OR 97321

541-928-8888

COW'S MILK

STYLES OF CHEESE

Fresh

Fromage Blanc

Soft-ripened

Camembert

Aged

Sublimity, plain and flavored

Oregonian Connie Collins, a film producer and wife of Australian film director George Miller, was inspired by the artisan-made cheeses she tasted Down Under—so inspired that she decided to get into the cheese business. She didn't have to look far to find a willing cheesemaker in nephew Brian Richter. He learned the art and craft of cheesemaking on a four-month apprenticeship alongside Fred Leppin of Top Paddock cheeses in the South Gippsland region of Australia. "Fred gave me an incredible education in making cheese," says Brian, "he taught me his cheesemaking secrets and gave me his blessing to use them here in Oregon."

And use them he did. Connie and Brian teamed up to start Oregon Gourmet Cheeses in 2002. The company is known for several styles of cheese, including a cow's milk Camembert-style cheese and Sublimity, an aged cheese, which Richter makes both plain and in combination with flavors such as the popular Herbes de Provence.

New owners acquired Oregon Gourmet in late 2007; Brian Richter remains at the cheesemaking helm. The new operating group has the eventual goal of expanding and diversifying production. Stay tuned for the next chapter of this developing cheese story.

6. SILVER FALLS CREAMERY

SHAWN HANOWELL AND FAMILY
1110 8th St. NE
Salem, OR 97301
503-551-5687
silverfallscreamery.com
GOAT'S MILK

Shawn Hanowell is a fourth-generation dairyman who has now become a cheesemaker

STYLES OF CHEESE
Fresh Chèvre, plain and flavored

We often forget that milk makes great cheese possible, and that good milk comes from animals that are healthy and well cared for. Shawn Hanowell, a fourth generation dairyman from Northwest Washington, is acutely aware of this fact. He started out keeping goats for a friend (they eventually became his), and, ever the herdsman, he started showing goats and became more serious about breeding and genetics. While managing animals is second nature for Shawn, he says that eventually it became clear that his goats needed to start paying for themselves instead of the other way around. Many cheesemakers will recognize the pattern: Shawn first experimented with recipes at home, hanging bags of chèvre to drain in the kitchen. The cheese was pretty good, and Silver Falls Creamery was officially up and running in 2004.

Today Shawn keeps his herd on a rented farm outside of Stayton, Oregon. He has around 90 milking goats, a mixed herd of Toggenbergs, Nubians, and Alpines, all carefully selected and bred for milk quality and production. He focuses primarily on making fresh chèvre, which he produces both plain and with several different flavorings, including jalapeno, rosemary, and lemon/dill; quite a feat considering he also has a wife, three children, and a full-time job working for the local school district.

7. WILLAMETTE VALLEY CHEESE COMPANY

ROD VOLBEDA

8105 Wallace Rd. NW

Salem, OR 97304

503-399-9806

wvcheeseco.com

COW AND SHEEP'S MILK

VISITORS

By appointment

STYLES OF CHEESE

Fresh

Queso Fresco

Soft-Ripened

French Prairie

Aged

Boerenkaas

Brindisi Fontina

Cheddar

Eola Jack

Havarti, plain and flavored

Gouda, plain and flavored

Mozzarella

Perrydale

Rod Volbeda makes cheeses that reflect his family's Dutch heritage

While he was a student at Oregon State University, Rod Volbeda spent a year in the Netherlands studying cheese production. After graduating, he put his cheesemaking knowledge to use in the lab at Tillamook County

Creamery. Later, he bought a dairy farm north of Salem, in the area where he grew up.

Once possessed with the cheese bug, Rod never really got rid of it. After tinkering with the idea of making cheese commercially for several years, experimenting with recipes, and acquiring equipment, he started Willamette Valley Cheese Company in 2002. Many area farmers watched this move with considerable skepticism. "A lot of people said I was nuts at the time," remembers Rod, but these days he's seen as a local pioneer who has set an example of ways dairies can develop value added products to diversify their businesses.

Today Rod Volbeda makes cheese from the milk of a substantial herd of Jersey cows that graze on the farm's certified organic pasture. More recently, he acquired a small herd of sheep to experiment with mixed milk cheeses, such as the popular Perrydale. Ever the student of cheese, he's still experimenting with cheese styles and varieties while dreaming of his next big project: underground aging caves.

A few of the Jersey cows whose milk goes into Willamette Valley Cheese Co.'s cheeses

NEW IN THE WILLAMETTE VALLEY

8. JACOBS CREAMERY

503-621-7910

jacobscreamery.com

Lisa Jacobs works in conjunction with Noris Dairy in Crabtree, Oregon, to produce a line of fresh cow's milk cheeses, including ricotta, mascarpone, and cream cheese. She's currently focused on selling locally to restaurants and at farmers' markets. "What I want to do is make varieties of cheese that you can't get anywhere else and make them really well," she says.

CENTRAL OREGON

9. JUNIPER GROVE FARM

PIERRE KOLISCH

2024 SW 58th St.

Redmond, OR 97756

541-923-8353

junipergrovefarm.com

GOAT'S MILK

Pierre Kolisch specializes in French-style goat's milk cheeses like this pyramid

STYLES OF CHEESE

Fresh

Feta

Fresh Chèvre, plain and flavored

Fromage blanc, plain and flavored

Thor's Special Smoked Crottin

Soft-Ripened

Buche Log

Dutchmen's Flat

Otentique

Pyramid

Silver Dollar

Aged

Cumin Tomme

Farmer's

Redmondo

Tumalo Tomme

Pierre Kolisch with Pat Morford of Rivers Edge Chévre at the annual Oregon Cheese Festival in Central Point, Oregon

After leaving his Southern California law practice in 1985, Portland native Pierre Kolisch spent two years in France learning cheesemaking. He first attended ENILBIO in Poligny and later apprenticed alongside several cheesemakers, including Francois Durand in Camembert. He eventually returned to the West Coast and purchased 5 acres in Redmond, Oregon, with aspirations of putting his newfound education to work making artisan cheeses.

Pierre had originally envisioned making cow's milk cheeses like those he had made in France, but that proved to be more difficult than he'd realized. "I couldn't find anyone to sell me milk," he says. Instead, he bought his own goats and today he's shepherd to a herd of over 100 milkers. Pierre also keeps a few pigs, which consume all of the whey left over after the cheesemaking process.

Many of the Northwest's early artisan cheesemakers blazed the trail for those coming later by introducing the idea of handcrafted artisan cheeses to wary consumers more familiar with mass produced varieties. Pierre developed his market the hard way, making numerous cold calls and selling retailers on the virtues of his products. Among his early supporters were Portland restaurateurs Greg Higgins, Vitaly Paley, and Cory Schreiber, a few of the core group of chefs responsible for revolutionizing Portland cuisine in the 1990s with their focus on seasonal, local ingredients—including artisan cheese. Now Pierre is a veteran of the cheesemaking business, and his handcrafted French-style cheeses are popular all over the country. The early challenge of turning consumers on to artisan cheese has turned into one of meeting growing demand.

10. TUMALO FARMS

FLAVIO AND MARGIE DeCASTILHOS

64515 Mock Rd.

Bend, OR 97701

541-350-3718

tumalofarms.com

GOAT'S MILK

STYLES OF CHEESE

Aged

Gouda-style goat cheeses, plain and flavored

Also makes styles for seasonal release, including Nocciola with hazelnuts, available in the fall, and Oregon Truffeleur, available in winter.

One of Tumalo Farms' curious goats

Many cheesemakers start out as farmers, while others come to the craft from the world of food or cooking. Flavio DeCastilhos may be the only domestic cheesemaker who found his way to cheesemaking by way of Silicon Valley. This veteran of the high-tech industry and a cofounder of Web MD was ready for a change when he decided on a cheese business as his next startup venture.

DeCastilhos initially intended to make sheep's milk cheeses, but difficulty

Flavio DeCastilhos sampling Tumalo Farms' cheeses

in finding the right sheep and post 9/11 restrictions on animal transport led him to goats instead. He purchased an old pumice mine on 80 acres outside of Bend, Oregon, and developed a goat farm and creamery. Open since 2005, Tumalo Farms has since grown to become Oregon's largest goat dairy, with over 300 animals and growing.

Tumalo Farms makes a variety of Gouda-style goat's milk cheeses, both plain and flavored. "My background led me into Gouda," says DeCastilhos. "While working in high-tech I spent a lot of time in Japan, where I got interested in Van Gogh, who was heavily influenced by Japanese art. During that time, I became really interested in Dutch culture." Later, when it came time to make cheese, Gouda was the obvious choice. DeCastilhos spent time in Holland learning about the cheese industry and making cheese; he also worked closely with Dutch experts when setting up his own plant.

DeCastilhos is as attuned to the business challenges inherent in artisan cheesemaking as he is to the quality of his cheeses. "Starting a cheese business resembles a high-tech startup. You spend a few years figuring out what works, then take it into production. You have to plan and market, develop the brand," he says. He has been spending the past several years doing just that. Ever-increasing demand, coupled with multiple awards for his cheeses, demonstrate that he's headed in the right direction.

OREGON COAST

11. ALSEA ACRE GOAT CHEESES

NANCY CHANDLER

PO Box 142

Alsea, OR 97324

888-316-4628

alseaacre.com

GOAT'S MILK

VISITORS

By appointment

Nancy Chandler shows off a few of her young goats

STYLES OF CHEESE

Fresh

> **Feta**
> **Fresh Chèvre, marinated in olive oil and herbs**
> **Fromage Blanc, plain and flavored**
> **Ricotta**

Former river-rafting guide and marketing manager Nancy Chandler was living on a small rented farm in Southern California when she became inspired by son Daniel's 4-H project raising goats. In 1994 she realized her dream when she purchased 2 acres in Alsea, Oregon, and turned her small herd of dairy goats into a full-time cheesemaking business. "When I started there were only two goat dairies in Oregon," she says. "Tall Talk Dairy closed soon after I started, so that left a niche at the right time for me to become established in the Oregon cheese market."

After 15 years of making cheese, Chandler is one of Oregon's long-established cheesemakers. Through experience, she's developed a rhythm, milking a herd of about 60 goats, making and selling cheese in the spring, summer, and fall, then taking a break in the winter when the goats are dry. A few quiet months of inactivity, watching and caring for gestating goats without the hustle and bustle of cheesemaking and selling is a welcome change for Nancy and her partner David Lygren.

Nancy focuses on making fresh goat cheeses; her fresh goat's milk ricotta and chèvre are much in demand by Portland restaurants and at local farmer's markets. Having established herself over the years, she doesn't see a need to make anything other than fresh cheese, the core of her success. "I just don't have time to age cheese," she says, "between making cheese and managing the goats and farmers' market sales, I'm plenty busy."

12. Rivers Edge Chèvre

Pat Morford

6315 Logsden Rd.

Logsden, OR 97537

541-444-1362

threeringfarm.com

GOAT'S MILK

VISITORS

*By appointment.
Holds an annual open house
during the summer; check the
Web site for details.*

STYLES OF CHEESE

Fresh

Confetti Moons

Fresh Chèvre, plain and flavored

Up in Smoke

Soft-Ripened

Full Moon

Heart's Desire

Old Flame

Petit Bonheur

**Pyramids, including Humbug
Mountain, Cape Foulweather,
and Mary's Peak**

Soft-Ripened continued

Siletz River Drums

Siletz River Stones

Sunset Bay

Valsetz

Yaquina Bay Pavé

Washed-Rind

Illahee

Mayor of Nye Beach

St. Olga

Three Ring Farm lies nestled amongst the hills east of the coastal town of Newport, Oregon. In this forested environment with a salty marine climate, Pat Morford, daughters Spring and Astraea, and a herd of 60 Alpine goats have been collaborating in the process of making exceptional goat cheese.

Pat has had goats most of her life. When she was a girl living on Vashon Island, Washington, her dad traded for three goats; Pinky, Stripes, and Jack cleared a lot of brush but ended up on the family dinner table. Eventually Pat started keeping goats herself. "Early on the goats were a way of having fresh milk for my family," she says. She made cheese for friends but the idea of running a cheese business was not in her mind—at least not yet.

Over the years Pat and partner, George, ran a commercial fishing business (George still fishes) in Newport out of their boat, the *Helen McColl*. In the late 1980s, they purchased 12 acres in Logsden and gradually began to acquire goats, breeding and selling them. Pat continued to make cheese informally while working as a chef at several local restaurants, including the Sylvia Beach Hotel. After securing a business loan and constructing a cheesemaking facility (and despite an absconding contractor), Rivers Edge Chèvre was born in 2005.

Pat Morford with daughter Astrea

Pat and her daughters make a range of gorgeous cheeses, from soft-ripened pyramids to washed-rind aged cheeses. One of her most popular products, Up in Smoke, is a delectable smoked chèvre wrapped in smoked maple leaves spritzed with bourbon that has taken the East Coast by storm, and was recently on *The Martha Stewart Show*. More recently, Pat has acquired a few sheep and plans to incorporate sheep's milk into her cheesemaking repertoire, something for cheese enthusiasts to look forward to.

13. TILLAMOOK COUNTY CREAMERY ASSOCIATION

DALE BAUMGARTNER, CHEESEMAKER

4175 Hwy. 101 North

Tillamook, OR 97141

503-815-1300

tillamookcheese.com

COW'S MILK

VISITORS

Tillamook's popular Visitors' Center is open year round, and features a self-guided tour. Hours vary by season; call ahead or check the Web site.

STYLES OF CHEESE

Fresh

Cheese curds

Aged

Cheddar (ranging from mild to sharp), including flavored and vintage

Colby

Aged continued

Monterey Jack

Mozzarella

Pepper Jack

Reduced Fat and Kosher Cheeses

Swiss

Also makes butter and ice cream

Though Tillamook is clearly no longer an artisan-scale cheesemaker, it has played a significant role in the history of regional cheesemaking. During the 19th century European immigrants migrated to Oregon's northern coast, which developed a reputation as a fertile valley conducive to cattle grazing. The remote location, rainy weather, and propensity to flooding, however, meant that the land was useful for little else. Eventually dozens of dairies established themselves in the area and a

COURTESY TILLAMOOK COUNTY CREAMERY ASSOCIATION

Blocks of cheddar make their way along Tillamook's efficient packaging line

cheesemaking industry developed as a means of preserving all of the milk being produced.

Peter McIntosh brought the original cheddar recipe (which is still in use today) to Tillamook in the 1890s and is credited with developing a consistently saleable product. By 1909, seven local cheesemakers banded together to establish a formal cheesemaking cooperative. The Tillamook brand evolved into one of the most recognizable cheese brands made on the West Coast during the early 20th century, leveraged by promotional campaigns such as the popular Tillamook Dairy Maid radio show. Over the ensuing decades, the remaining cheese factories in the area consolidated under the Tillamook banner.

Oregon's oldest existing cheesemaker, Tillamook has over its 100 years become Oregon's largest cheesemaker as well. In 1999 Tillamook expanded its operation considerably when it opened a second manufacturing plant in the Eastern Oregon town of Boardman. Tillamook's early settlers and cheesemakers would no doubt be surprised to learn that the industry they struggled to develop now produces over 120 million pounds of cheese a year and its products are sold in all 50 states.

SOUTHERN OREGON

14. PHOLIA FARM

GIANACLIS AND VERN CALDWELL

9115 W Evans Creek Rd.

Rogue River, OR 97537

541-582-8883

pholiafarm.com

GOAT'S MILK

STYLES OF CHEESE

Aged

Covered Bridge

Elk Mountain

Hillis Peak

Washed-Rind

Wimer Winter

Pholia Farm bustles with the activity of 60 energetic goats. But look a little closer and you'll notice something different: these dairy goats are adorably cute Nigerian Dwarf goats, the pint-sized version of a "normal" goat, standing less than 2 feet tall. While these goats are small enough to be kept for pets, this breed's milk is especially high in protein and butterfat, more than twice the butterfat of regular goat's milk, making it perfect for cheesemaking. In fact, Pholia Farm is among the first cheesemaking operations in the United States making cheese from the milk of Nigerian Dwarf goats.

Vern and Gianaclis Caldwell purchased their first few Nigerian Dwarf goats while living

31

Nigerian dwarf goat kids are just about the cutest things you'll ever see

in San Diego County, California. "I had dairy cows growing up and initially wanted to provide healthy, kindly raised milk for our family," Gianaclis says. She happened to come across a magazine article about dairy goats that mentioned the Nigerian Dwarf breed; it appealed to her, in part, because daughter Amelia, then eight years old, would be able to handle them easily. Soon enough, the family was experimenting with using goat's milk to make various products, including soap and cheese.

While it's a long way from Southern California to Southern Oregon, the move was actually a homecoming of sorts for Gianaclis, who was raised on the land where Pholia Farm now lies. The Caldwells have developed a self-sustaining farm and cheesemaking operation that fuels itself exclusively with energy from solar panels and a micro-hydro turbine, with a biodiesel generator for emergencies. "Vern and I are bothered by the consumption and consumerism going on in the United States . . . while we may not make much of a dent in that, we can try!" says Gianaclis. Plans are currently in the works for an underground aging cellar, which will make room for even more of Pholia's outstanding cheeses.

15. ROGUE CREAMERY

DAVID GREMMELS AND CARY BRYANT

311 N Front St.

Central Point, OR 97502

541-665-1155

roguecreamery.com

COW AND GOAT'S MILK

Blue Cheese has been made at Rogue Creamery since 1957

STYLES OF CHEESE

Fresh

Cheese curds, available at the shop

Aged

Cheddar, plain and flavored
Touvelle

Blue

Crater Lake Blue
Echo Mountain Blue *(cow and goat's milk blend)*
Oregon Blue
Oregonzola
Rogue River Blue *(available seasonally)*
Smokey Blue

Tom Vella, owner of Vella Cheese Company in Sonoma, California, purchased what was then Rogue River Valley Creamery Cooperative in 1935. He built a thriving business supplying bulk cheddar cheese to

David Gremmels (left) and Cary Bryant, owners of Rogue Creamery

Kraft and later to the military during WWII. Vella eventually acquired and ran several other cheesemaking facilities in the area, including Rogue Gold Creamery in nearby Grant's Pass.

Production began to wane during the 1970s and 1980s as local dairies went out of business and cheese production shifted to urban centers. By 2002, Tom's son, Ig Vella, was on the verge of closing what was then called Rogue River Valley Creamery, the last of Vella's plants still in operation in Southern Oregon. Enter David Gremmels, then a marketing executive at Harry & David in nearby Medford, and Cary Bryant, a microbiologist and successful entrepreneur, who were exploring the possibility of establishing a wine bar in nearby Ashland, Oregon. They met with Vella about the possibility of carrying Rogue's cheeses at their establishment but soon found that Vella had other plans. "Ig was closing the creamery in three weeks when we met with him," says Gremmels. "He had other offers but he didn't want to just sell the brand, he really wanted to sell to someone who could sustain the company." Gremmels and Bryant found themselves shaking hands with Vella, and on July 1, 2002 they became artisan cheesemakers.

Rogue Creamery's history is in part reflected in the varieties of blue cheese it produces. The first evolved in the 1950s after Tom Vella visited Roquefort, France. Inspired by what he saw, he returned to Oregon and began to produce the original Oregon Brand Blue Vein Cheese (later shortened to Oregon Blue) starting in 1957. Oregonzola, the creamery's

second-generation blue cheese, was developed by Ig Vella as a tribute to his late father in 1998. It is created in the style of an Italian Gorgonzola, using proprietary molds from Italy. After acquiring the company, Gremmels and Bryant developed the third-generation blue, Crater Lake Blue. "We wanted to create a rich, broadly profiled blue that had depth and creaminess," says Gremmels, an effect they achieved by mixing several strains of blue molds from France, Italy, and Denmark. Finding a name was easy. "We wanted a name that spoke to all the shades of blue that come out when you see it," says Gremmels. Nearby Crater Lake, known for the intensity of its deep blue waters, was a natural choice. Gremmels and Bryant also developed the creamery's signature Rogue River Blue, a seasonal blue aged with a natural rind, then wrapped in local grape leaves that have been macerated in pear brandy.

Gremmels and Bryant have continued the spirit and tradition of entrepreneurship established by Tom and Ig Vella. Their quality cheeses, innovative marketing and leadership in the cheesemaking community have propelled Rogue Creamery into the forefront of artisan cheesemaking in the United States. In 2007 Rogue Creamery became the first artisan cheesemaker in the United States to export raw-milk cheese to the European Union.

COURTESY ROGUE CREAMERY

Nearby Rogue View Dairy supplies all of the milk that goes into Rogue Creamery's cheeses

16. SISKIYOU CREST GOAT DAIRY

MOOKIE MOSS AND STU O'NEILL

5758 Sterling Creek Rd.
Jacksonville, OR 97530
541-899-1694

GOAT'S MILK

VISITORS
By appointment

When Siskiyou Crest founder Mookie Moss gives the call, the goats come in for milking

STYLES OF CHEESE

Fresh

Feta

Fresh Chèvre

Aged

Cheddar

Mike Moss didn't grow up imagining himself as a farmer, much less a cheese-maker, but the vocation snuck up on him and now he wouldn't have it any other way. A Colorado native, Moss accumulated valuable experience interning on farms from California to Upstate New York before settling in Southern Oregon.

After purchasing a farm in the Applegate Valley near Jacksonville, Mike (who goes by the nickname Mookie) started a produce-growing operation as a member of the Siskiyou Sustainable Co-op; he still farms about 3 acres of vegetables and herbs. But because of the farm's remote location, steep slopes, and limited water supply, he knew he would eventually need to look for additional ways to generate income. Drawing on prior goat-keeping experience, he acquired several milking goats; by mid-2007, he had developed a licensed cheesemaking operation.

East coast native Stu O'Neill, a community organizer and veteran of the restaurant industry, also lives and works on the farm, bringing a wealth of marketing and business experience to the operation. He came to Southern Oregon to go to

Stu O'Neill (left) and Mookie Moss

college and ended up staying, now farming and helping to manage the creamery business.

Boones Farm, named after Mookie's 11-year-old hound and chief farm caretaker, currently supports a herd of about 50 goats, 20 or so milking at any given time. Both men milk the goats by hand during the season with the help of a rotating group of interns. In addition to farming, Mookie and Stu are committed to creating a strong rural economy and community as well as social and environmental justice.

NEW IN SOUTHERN OREGON

17. NEW MOON GOAT DAIRY

LYNNE AND JENNY CABRAL

21910 Sprague River Rd.
Chiloquin, OR 97624
541-533-2487

Lynne Cabral has lived in Southern Oregon for over 30 years, ranching and grazing cattle on 1,000 acres of pastureland in the Klamath Basin. She had entertained the idea of making and selling cheese for years, but finally realized that dream in the summer of 2008 when she was licensed to make cheese from the milk of her herd of about 100 goats. Currently Lynne and daughter Jenny are concentrating on making fresh chèvres and tortes, which they sell at the farmers' market in Klamath Falls, Oregon.

CHAPTER 2

WASHINGTON

Seattle / Puget Sound

Southwest Washington • *Northwest Washington*

Central / Eastern Washington

SEATTLE/PUGET SOUND

1. BEECHER'S HANDMADE CHEESE

KURT DAMMEIER

BRAD SINKO, CHEESEMAKER

1600 Pike Place

Seattle, WA 98101

206-956-1964

beechershandmadecheese.com

COW'S MILK

VISITORS

Open 9 AM–6 PM, daily

Beecher's Flagship Reserve must be carefully maintained during the aging process

STYLES OF CHEESE

Fresh

Blank Slate *(fromage blanc)*

Cheese Curds

Aged

Beecher's Flagship and Flagship Reserve

Marco Polo and Marco Polo Reserve

Monterey Jack, plain and flavored

Whether you call him a businessman or a cheese evangelist, you'll have to agree that Kurt Dammeier turned Seattle on to cheese when he opened Beecher's Handmade Cheese in 2003. "I love cheese and I'm just Type A enough to want to make my own," he laughs. Now over five years later, the popular and visitor friendly shop in Seattle's Pike Place Market is turning out qual-

40

Flagship Reserve, a cloth-wrapped version of Beecher's popular Flagship cheese, debuted in 2006

ity cheese that has translated into staying power for this urban creamery.

Dammeier, a fourth-generation Puget Sounder who grew up in the Tacoma area, has been interested in food all his life. He started cooking as a kid, tweaking his mom's cinnamon toast technique, and later deciding he preferred Tillamook Cheddar to Kraft singles. No surprise, then, that this self-styled food entrepreneur and chef would grew up to become involved in the food business and publish a cookbook, *Pure Flavor,* in 2007.

Beecher's cheesemaker, Brad Sinko, has been with the company since it started. He came to Beecher's from Bandon Cheese Company in Bandon, Oregon, the company his family owned until 2002, when it was sold to Tillamook. Beecher's first made three vats of cheese per week; Seattle responded favorably, and now production is up to two times per day, seven days a week, using milk trucked in from two farms east of Seattle near Duvall, Washington.

While Beecher's makes several styles of cheese, its mainstay, Flagship, has been successful at least in part because of its broad appeal to consumers and cheese aficionados alike. The cheddar-style cheese with a Gruyere twist is made several ways: in its regular aged format (aged 18–20 months) and as Flagship Reserve, which is cave-aged in 40-pound wheels called *truckles* in the manner of an Old World Cheddar. Flagship Reserve took Second Place overall in a field of over 1,200 cheeses at the American Cheese Society Competition in 2007.

2. ESTRELLA FAMILY CREAMERY

KELLI AND ANTHONY ESTRELLA

659 Wynoochee Valley Rd.

Montesano, WA 98563

360-249-6541

estrellafamilycreamery.com

COW AND GOAT'S MILK

VISITORS

*Farm store open
Saturdays, 10 AM–4 PM,
or by appointment*

STYLES OF CHEESE

Soft-Ripened

Partly Sunny

Reposee

Subblime

Aged

Black Creek Buttery

Dominoes

Grisdale Goat

Jalapeno Buttery

Killeen

Weebles

Washed-Rind

Bea Truffled

Brewleggio

Caldwell Crik Chèvrette

(cow/goat's milk blend)

Guapier

Old Apple Tree Tomme

Red Darla

Valentina

Vineyard Tome

Blue

Wynoochee River Blue

Kelli Estrella is a dreamer. She didn't grow up on a farm, but she knew she wanted to have cows. Kelli and Anthony married 23 years ago, and eventually they purchased a 164-acre farm outside of Montesano, about 30 miles from the Central Washington coast. The former dairy with verdant pastures was a natural place to start raising animals for making cheese. Today the farm supports a herd of 24 Normande cows and about 50 goats. From Kelli's initial inspiration, the Estrellas have built an award-winning artisan cheese operation crafting outstanding farmstead, raw-milk cheeses.

Kelli and Anthony make the farm run with the help of six adopted children (three from war-ravaged Liberia) who all contribute to making the farm run smoothly. Kelli will tell you that the two boys, Samuel and Ernest, are most comfortable working the animals, while Ruth and the other girls, Faith, Melody, and Patience, stick closer to the creamery, but everyone contributes wherever there's work to do, and there's always work to do on a farm this size.

Estrella is known for both the variety of cheeses she makes as well as their complex quality. Where few regional cheesemakers experiment with more technical styles of cheese, like washed-rind or blue cheeses, Kelli is at once fear-

Estrella Family Creamery has won multiple national and international awards for its outstanding cheeses

Kelli and daughter Ruth are the chief cheesemakers of the Estrella family

less and brilliant. Her Caldwell Crick Chèvrette, a mixed goat and cow's milk washed-rind cheese, is one of the most exceptional examples of a washed-rind cheese available in the Pacific Northwest. Her cheeses are that good—and getting even better. In 2006 the Estrellas formally christened a new cheese cave, Cave Beulah, one of only a few underground cheese-aging caves in the Pacific Northwest. The cave has allowed Estrella more room to hold aging cheese and has contributed to the flavor profile and consistency of her products.

3. MT. TOWNSEND CREAMERY

WILL O'DONNELL, MATT DAY, AND RYAN TRAIL

338 Sherman St.

Port Townsend, WA 98368

360-379-0895

mttownsendcreamery.com

COW'S MILK

Matt Day (left), Will O' Donnell (center), and Ryan Trail

STYLES OF CHEESE

Soft-Ripened

Cirrus

Seastack

Aged

Trailhead

Will O' Donnell, Matt Day, and Ryan Trail arrived in Port Townsend, Washington, separately but came together serendipitously to realize a common goal: making cheese. Will, a self-described recovering artist with an organic farm, had been working with a local farmer, ultimately unsuccessfully, to develop a farmstead cheesemaking facility. Around the same time, friends Matt and Ryan had been investigating local business opportunities, including artisan cheesemaking. When Ryan and Will met while taking a childbirth class with their wives, the mutual pursuits eventually dovetailed into an unexpected but fortuitous birth, that of Mt. Townsend Creamery.

After experimenting with a variety of recipes, Mt. Townsend began making and selling cheese in 2006. Their milk comes from two local dairies (combining mixed Holstein and Brown Swiss genetics) and they make two soft-ripened and one aged cheese, the Trailhead. After a quick start selling locally at the Port Townsend Farmers' Market, demand has taken off and Mt. Townsend's products are currently available across the Northwest. Their Seastack, a soft-ripened cheese dusted with ash and modeled after the French Chaource, has been particularly popular. After a modest plant expansion in late 2007, success and future growth is Mt. Townsend's latest adventure.

Mt. Townsend Creamery Trailhead ages for at least three months before it's released

4. PORT MADISON FARM

STEVE AND BEVERLY PHILLIPS

15015 Sunrise Dr. NE

Bainbridge Island, WA 98110

206-842-4125

GOAT'S MILK

STYLES OF CHEESE

Fresh

Fresh Chèvre, plain and flavored

Aged

Cheddar

Gruyere

Mozzarella

Spring Cheese *(Havarti style)*

Also sells goat's milk and yogurt

Steve and Beverly Phillips came to cheesemaking from diverse professions—he from furniture manufacturing and she from the computer industry (though she'd grown up on a farm). "I knew I wanted to be a farmer when Beverly made me my first omelette with range-fed eggs," Steve laughs. He was a quick convert to the farming life. Over the years, the Phillips have raised a variety of produce and animals at their farm at the north end of Bainbridge Island, including poultry, pigs, and organic vegetables.

Cheese entered their lives somewhat accidentally; Beverly bred a pet goat and produced a milker so exceptional that the goat was ranked among the top producers nationally. And an idea was born. "At first we thought we'd just sell milk," says Steve, "but I made a little cheese on the side and fell in love with cheesemaking." One of Washington's longest running cheesemakers, Port Madison Farm has been making and selling goat's milk and farmstead cheeses since 1985.

Steve acquired the craft by taking a number of classes, including the WSU course, as well as spending time working with cheesemakers in France. While there, he was impressed by the regional sense of place and character communicated by the cheese and shared by the local community. "That's one reason we've focused exclusively on selling locally," he says. "I'm more interested in what makes this region special, developing that kind of regionality."

The Phillipses have been in the farming and cheesemaking business for several decades and are now beginning to think about the future. While many new cheesemakers focus on future expansion, these veterans are currently working their way in the opposite direction. "Each year we've been getting

smaller instead of bigger," says Steve. They've cut their goat herd to 65 milking Nubians, down from over 100 several years ago. As a result, production has slowed a bit and Steve says he's making fewer aged cheeses than in the past.

5. QUAIL CROFT FARMSTEAD GOAT CHEESE

ALAYNE SUNDBERG

2553A Cattle Point Rd.

Friday Harbor, WA 98250

360-378-5764

GOAT'S MILK

STYLES OF CHEESE
Fresh Chèvre, plain and flavored

These goats have a view. Quail Croft's 40 goats, mostly Saanen and Saanen crosses, graze in a beautiful pasture on San Juan Island overlooking Griffin Bay and adjacent Lopez Island. On a clear day they can see Mt. Baker, but they're usually occupied with more important matters, particularly grazing.

Layne Sundberg has had goats for most of the past 30 years in several locations, including Kodiak, Alaska, and on San Juan Island. She made cheese informally for many years, for herself and friends, finally weathering the somewhat arduous licensing process and becoming official in 2005. "Many of the rules were developed for large industrial operations," she says, "so it was tough for me to fit into the mold." But fit in she has, to the delight of island residents and chefs.

Alayne Sundberg

Quail Croft's goats have a gorgeous view of Puget Sound

Sundberg's fresh chèvre is a boutique product available primarily at the San Juan Island Farmers' Market and local restaurants, as well as on Lopez and Orcas Island. Even so, she struggles to keep up with growing demand. She manages her entire operation singlehandedly, from milking to goatkeeping to cheesemaking, a routine that she says can be exhausting, but satisfying as well. She believes deeply in the importance of caring for the land and animals, practices that she knows will lead to good milk and good cheese.

6. River Valley Ranch

Rob and Julie Steil

34920 SE Fall City-Snoqualmie Rd.

Fall City, WA 98024

425-222-5277

rivervalleycheese.com

Goat, Cow, and Water Buffalo's Milk

STYLES OF CHEESE

Fresh

Fresh Chèvre, plain and flavored

Fresh Mozzarella *(made with both Water Buffalo and Cow's milk)*

Aged Cow's Milk

BoVino

Naughty Nellie

Pepper Jack

Valley Girl

Aged Goat's Milk

Calamity Jane

Ranch Reserve

Silly Billy

Valley Doe

River Valley Ranch is located about 30 miles east of Seattle

*L*ike many cheesemakers, Julie Steil didn't plan to make cheese for a living. A native of the South who still sports a slight southern drawl, this former model and Seattle commercial real estate developer initially took up

cheesemaking as a hobby. Her experimentation turned more serious when she realized that the cheese she was making was pretty good; from there, things have really taken off. What was originally a retirement project has instead turned into a successful and expanding business.

The farm's first project was selling raw milk (legal in Washington if sold by licensed facilities) while the first cheeses were aging. Next, Julie and husband Rob started selling cheese at local farmers' markets, drawing raves particularly for their fresh chèvres with flavorings, including herbs, figs, and jalapenos. Today River Valley Ranch makes more than 20 styles of fresh and aged cheeses from cow and goat's milk as well as a true buffalo mozzarella from their small herd of water buffalo.

Puget Sound chefs have taken notice, and Julie says restaurants are now one of their most ardent supporters. In a neat bit of symbiosis, River Valley Ranch partners

Julie Steil at the Seattle Cheese Festival, held annually at Seattle's famous Pike Place Market

with fellow artisans at Pike Brewing Company in Seattle, using the spent barley from beer-making to feed their animals, and in turn making a cheese, Naughty Nellie, that's washed with the brewery's beer. The popularity of their cheeses coupled with the Steils' marketing savvy has turned River Valley Ranch into a strong presence in Northwest cheesemaking.

7. SEA BREEZE FARM

GEORGE PAGE
10730 SW 116th
Vashon Island, WA 98070
206-567-5769
COW'S MILK
Also at:
LA BOUCHERIE (RETAIL OUTLET)
17635 100th Ave. SW
Vashon Island, WA 98070
206-567-4628
seabreezefarm.net

VISITORS

*La Boucherie open
9 AM–7 PM; closed
Sunday and Monday*

STYLES OF CHEESE

Fresh
Ricotta

Aged
Vache de Vashon
Vasheron

Also sells bottled milk

George Page thinks in terms of cycles. "Our cows give milk, which goes into cheese. But the cows also fertilize the pasture, as do our chickens. We eat eggs from the chickens, as well as the meat. And the whey from making cheese goes to our pigs, which we also eat and make into various things, such as cured meats and prosciutto." Cheesemaking is but one aspect of the grand integrated scheme that is Sea Breeze Farm.

George and his wife, Kristin, own about 10 acres that make up the core of Sea Breeze Farm on the north end of Vashon Island, not far as the crow flies from downtown Seattle. In addition, George also uses and manages multiple additional plots of land all over the island (totaling about 80 acres) where he keeps sheep and pigs and rotates pastures. He says the farming life sort of snuck up on him while he was in college. As a physics major, he got interested in cooking and soon realized that good cooking could only really happen with good ingredients. One thing led to another, and soon he and his wife were raising chickens at their condo in Seattle's Queen Anne Hill neighborhood for the eggs. He says he thought about getting goats then as well, but soon realized that his vision of farming was growing into something more than just a backyard hobby. He and Kristin purchased their farm on Vashon Island in 2000 (Kristin grew up on Vashon and her parents still live there) and Sea Breeze Farm has grown from there.

In the past, George made cheese from both goat and cow's milk, but he's focusing solely on cow's milk cheeses these days: Vache de Vashon, a Gruyere-style tomme, and the Vasheron, a harder grateable cheese, aged as long as a year or more. Those who visit Sea Breeze Farm at local farmers' markets may also be able to enjoy their fresh ricotta, available seasonally. George's most recent project is a retail shop and small restaurant located in downtown Vashon, called La Boucherie, which he hopes to develop into both a neighborhood hub and a place to make and sell many of his cured meats, pates, and wine as well as cheese.

8. STEAMBOAT ISLAND GOAT FARM

JASON DREW

9201 Steamboat Island Rd. NW

Olympia, WA 98502

360-866-8568

steamboatislandgoatfarm.com

GOAT'S MILK

STYLES OF CHEESE

Fresh

Feta

Aged

Cheddar

Jack

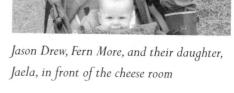

Jason Drew and Fern More live on a 6-acre plot of land outside of Olympia overlooking Totten Inlet, part of southern Puget Sound. Along with their new daughter, Jaela, they're developing a farm around an orchard, chickens, and farmstead raw-milk cheeses made from the milk of their herd of 18 or so goats.

Jason knows the area well, having spent many hours as a kid visiting his grandparents' beach house in the Steamboat Island area, a gorgeous peninsula in South Puget Sound. After getting his Master's in Public Administration at the University of Washington, he spent time in India at a Slow Food conference hosted by Navdanya, an NGO founded by Vandana Shiva held at the Bija Vidyapeeth Center on Nav-

Jason Drew, Fern More, and their daughter, Jaela, in front of the cheese room

Steamboat Island
Goat Farm

Jason Drew makes several aged cheeses, including Monterey Jack and cheddar (in black wax)

Steamboat Island's goats graze on verdant pasture during the spring and summer

danya's organic farm. He continued to travel in India before returning to Washington. He met Fern while volunteering at the Olympia Food Co-op, where she works, and today they're building a family as well as a farm.

After starting up, Jason spent about a year keeping goats and experimenting with the finer points of making cheese. By April of 2006, he was officially licensed to sell cheese commercially. While he initially sold a fair amount of raw goat's milk this year he's concentrating almost exclusively on using all of his milk to make cheese. Along with help from volunteer cheesemaker Cathy Harding, he's now focused on establishing a range of cheeses that work with his milk and express the terroir of the area. One of Jason's long-term goals is to get the farm off petroleum products and to be as energy independent as possible.

SOUTHWEST WASHINGTON

9. BLACK SHEEP CREAMERY

BRAD AND MEG GREGORY

PO Box 293

Adna, WA 98522

360-520-3397

blacksheepcreamery.com

SHEEP'S MILK

Black Sheep Creamery

STYLES OF CHEESE

Fresh

Feta

Fresh Sheep's Milk Cheese

Ricotta

Aged

Black Sheep Tomme

Mopsy's Best

Queso de Oveja

Brad and Meg Gregory moved to their farm, gorgeous land adjacent to the Chehalis River, in 1993. They started out raising crops, but when their second son developed an allergy to milk, they acquired a few sheep and experimented with milking them. Soon they had extra milk on their hands and began to wonder what else they might do with it, thus the idea to make sheep's-milk cheese was formed. This eventually evolved into Black Sheep Creamery, which opened in 2005.

Brad is an engineer by training. Meg was initially the family cheesemaker, but they soon realized that her "real" job as a public health nurse (with benefits) was important to retain, so Brad assumed full-time cheesemaking duties. Brad makes cheese in the farm's old cow milking parlor that he converted to a cheesemaking facility. Particularly popular has been Mopsy's

Best, an aged tomme named after one of the family's original sheep; it took Second Place in its category at the 2007 American Cheese Society Competition.

The Gregorys' fortunes turned in December of 2007, when the Chehalis River flooded, causing extensive damage throughout Southwest Washington. Floodwaters inundated their property and cheesemaking operation; most of their sheep perished in the flood, and while the barn and facilities survived, their cheesemaking equipment was damaged by several feet of mud and water. Today Brad and Meg are doing double duty, making cheese as well as rebuilding their home, farm, and flock. As Meg says, they are working hard and looking forward, "Onward and upward, out of the muck!" During 2008 the Gregorys were up and running, selling cheese at farmers' markets and to retailers and restaurants in the Portland and Seattle areas. Their courage and perseverance have been an inspiration.

10. BLUE ROSE DAIRY

RHONDA AND DAVID RIDER

123 Rayburn Rd. W

Winlock, WA 98596

360-785-0319

bluerosedairy.com

GOAT'S MILK

VISITORS
By appointment

STYLES OF CHEESE

Fresh

Feta

Fresh Chèvre, plain and flavored

Aged

Black Jewels

Grande Rosa

Northwest Comfort

Rhonda Rider is a busy woman; juggling multiple responsibilities as a mother, foster mother, and homeschooler keeps her moving. These days, a good portion of her time also goes to making cheese from the milk of her herd of more than 100 dairy goats.

Rhonda and her husband, David, acquired their first goat prior to 2000. "My kids didn't like goat's milk," Rhonda laughs, "so I started to make cheese to do something with it." Over time, Rhonda experimented with cheesemaking, and by 2003 the family decided to take the plunge into full-time farming, purchasing a 13-acre former goat dairy near Winlock, Washington. While they readily admit they went into the project without much goatkeeping knowledge, the family successfully weathered the trials and

Rhonda and David Rider

tribulations and became licensed as a goat dairy in 2004.

Initially the family sold milk to a local processing facility and made cheese at nearby Black Sheep Creamery. Blue Rose Dairy became licensed to make cheese at the farm in 2007, and Rhonda makes cheese full time during the season. Daughters Ali and Danyel help out where they can, milking goats and packaging and labeling cheese. Eventually, Rhonda and her husband hope to develop a bed-and-breakfast on the farm for visitors to stay and experience rural farm living.

11. TWIN OAKS CREAMERY

GARY AND HEATHER HOWELL

346 Twin Oaks Rd.

Chehalis, WA 98532

360-748-6788

COW AND GOAT'S MILK

STYLES OF CHEESE

Fresh

Fresh Chèvre, plain and flavored

Fresh Mozzarella *(cow's milk)*

Soft-ripened

Brie *(cow's milk)*

Aged

Smoked Mozzarella *(cow's milk)*

Blue

Chehalis Blue *(cow's milk)*

Also sells bottled milk and butter

Twin Oaks Creamery
Milk & Farmstead Cheese
Gary & Heather Howell
360-748-6788

Heather Howell had been making cheese for several years prior to the storms that hit Southwest Washington in December 2007. Like other farmers in the area, including nearby Black Sheep Creamery, the Howells suffered tremendous damage in the flooding, losing most of their animals as well as about 500 pounds of stored cheese. Visitors to the Olympia Farmers' Market were excited to see Twin Oaks Creamery return in 2008 with a diverse line of cheeses, including soft-ripened cow's-milk brie, blue cheese, and fresh chèvres. Aged cheeses will return soon as well, and with any luck these resourceful folks will continue to prosper.

NEW IN SOUTHWEST WASHINGTON

12. DEE CREEK FARM

MIKE AND ANITA PUCKETT
PO Box 1936
Woodland, WA 98674
360-225-9711
deecreekfarm.com
COW, GOAT, AND SHEEP'S MILK

Dee Creek Farm is a diverse farming operation offering chickens, lamb, and produce for sale; most recently cheese has joined the repertoire of offerings. Anita Puckett, Dee Creek's cheesemaker, started out making a raw goat's milk feta, which they've been selling at the Vancouver Farmers' Market and through local CSA distribution. Anita looks forward to developing more styles of cheese in the future, including mixed milk cheeses made with goat, cow, and sheep's milk.

13. ROSECREST FARM

GARY AND SHARON MCCOOL
439 Spooner Rd.
Chehalis, WA 98532

360-740-8988
rosecrestfarm.org
COW'S MILK

Gary and Sharon McCool have been in the dairy business for over 25 years, milking a herd of about 130 Milking Shorthorn cows. Sharon says Gary had always wanted to try making cheese; when they found someone eager to sell used equipment, they jumped at the chance, and became officially licensed to make cheese in early 2008. Sharon, the family cheesemaker, plans to focus on making Swiss-style cheeses, both plain and flavored.

14. WILLAPA HILLS FARMSTEAD CHEESE

*STEPHEN HUEFFED
AND AMY TURNBULL*
PO Box 274
Doty, WA 98539

206-612-6253
willapahillsfarmsteadcheese.com
COW AND SHEEP'S MILK

Stephen Hueffed and Amy Turnbull moved to rural Doty, Washington, from the Puget Sound area several years ago along with their three young children and started a sheep dairy. They're currently milking about 120 sheep (and growing) and a few Jersey cows and busily developing a line of cheeses with a decided emphasis on blue cheese. Plans include a fresh sheep's milk ricotta and an aged blue called Ewe Moon.

NORTHWEST WASHINGTON

15. APPEL FARMS

JOHN AND RICH APPEL

6605 Northwest Rd.

Ferndale, WA 98248

360-312-1431

appel-farms.com

COW'S MILK

VISITORS

Open Monday–Saturday,
9 AM–6 PM

Friday afternoons are popular at
Appel Farms—for obvious reasons

STYLES OF CHEESE

Fresh

Cheese Curds, plain and flavored

Feta

Fromage Blanc

Paneer

Quark

Aged

Cheddar, plain and flavored

Gouda, plain and flavored

Jack Appel, a native of Holland, learned to make cheese while on a two-year apprenticeship in France with a Dutch farmer. He later immigrated to the United States and eventually settled on a farm in the Ferndale area of Northwest Washington in the 1960s. Appel made Gouda as a hobby

63

Gouda-making day at Appel Farms

for many years, selling mostly to family and friends around the holidays; the original wooden tub and press that Appel imported from Holland and used during the early days are on display in the farm shop.

As it turned out, Quark (a thick yogurt-style cheese) rather than Gouda led the Appel family toward a full-fledged cheesemaking business. "A German man came to the farm and asked my dad if he'd make Quark," says John Appel, Jack's son. "He was also an immigrant and he'd been selling pickled herring and other ethnic products to German delis along the coast." The niche product clicked, and today Appel Farm's Quark is distributed nationally. Their other specialty product, Indian-style Paneer, developed in a similar way: a native of India asked the Appels if they were interested in making and selling it. Now it's one of Appel Farm's top selling products.

Jack Appel has since passed away and his sons, John and Rich, have taken over the farm and family business. John currently manages the cheesemaking side and Rich runs the 200 Holstein cow dairy. John restarted Gouda production about five years ago with the help of British Columbia cheesemaker Arie Gort, and hopes to grow that area of their production in the future, a move that brings the Appel family full circle, back to their Dutch roots.

16. EL MICHOACANO

GABRIEL MONTES DE OCA

6408 52nd NE

Marysville, WA 98270

360-658-0914

COW'S MILK

STYLES OF CHEESE

Fresh

Crema

Panela

Queso Fresco

Requeson

El Michoacano makes Hispanic-style cheeses from Jersey cows' milk. Their products are distributed locally to restaurants and small markets in the Everett and Marysville area.

17. GOLDEN GLEN CREAMERY

VIC AND JUDY JENSEN

15098 Field Rd.

Bow, WA 98232

360-766-6455

goldenglencreamery.com

COW'S MILK

STYLES OF CHEESE

Fresh

Cheese Curds

Feta

Mozzarella

Aged

Cheddar in Medium, Sharp, and Extra Sharp, also flavored

Gouda in Medium, Old, and Very Old

Also sells bottled milk and butter

If you're driving in the Skagit Valley toward Bow, Washington, and Golden Glen Creamery, you'll see the big blue silo well before you arrive. That's a relic from the old days, when dairy farmers Vic and Judy Jensen started their dairy and were milking Guernsey cows—the silo still bears the name of their old farm, Golden Glen Guernseys. The Jensens were eventually forced to change breeds when the bank wouldn't lend them money unless they switched to Holsteins, the dairy industry standard due

GOLDEN GLEN CREAMERY

Natural Handcrafted Cheese Produced by the Jensen Ladies
15098 Field Road · Bow, Washington 98232
www.goldenglencreamery.com
360.766.MILK

to their high milk-producing capacity. At its high point, their dairy had over 400 cows.

Dairy farming is a difficult business; many dairy families have difficulty maintaining their livelihood in the face of unstable milk prices and skyrocketing feed costs. One idea that the Jensens came up with, as a solution for these issues, was to make cheese from some of their milk, a value-added product with the potential to increase the dairy's bottom

Gouda aging gracefully at Golden Glen Creamery

line. After taking cheesemaking classes at Cal State in San Luis Obispo, the Jensen Ladies, as Judy and her daughter-in-law Brandy call themselves, started making cheese in 2004. Now, almost five years later, Golden Glen Creamery is down to a more sustainable 75 cows, including a few Guernseys, and it turns out farmstead cheese, butter, and premium bottled milk with great success.

18. GOTHBERG FARMS

RHONDA GOTHBERG

15203 Sunset Rd.

Bow, WA 98232

360-202-2436

gothbergfarms.com

VISITORS

By appointment

STYLES OF CHEESE

Fresh

Feta

Fresh Chèvre, plain and flavored

Ricotta

Yogurt

Soft-Ripened

Mt. Baker Ash

Aged

Caerphilly

Cheddar

Gouda, plain and flavored

Parmesan

After a career as a nurse executive, Rhonda Gothberg was ready for something else. "I wanted a family goat for a little home milk, a few chickens, a little home cheese," she laughs. One mother–baby goat pair turned into several more and several more . . . and now Gothberg finds herself with a milking herd of 14 LaMancha goats, along with a thriving cheesemaking business. She's the kind of person whose energy and enthusiasm leaves little doubt that she'd be successful at whatever she put her mind to.

The move to farming and goatkeeping was not a big change for Gothberg, a Texas native. Her family had gardens and chickens when she was growing up and she and her brother spent time on the farms of extended family. Much later, when she acquired goats herself, she found that the skills acquired during her nursing career translated perfectly. "Nursing is part art and part science, and cheesemaking and goat herdsmanship is all the same thing. I know something about chemistry, I understood anatomy and physiology, I'm not afraid to give shots, I know how to listen for heartbeat. Everything just clicked for me." Now Rhonda splits her time running successful two businesses: real estate and artisan cheesemaking.

Gothberg and several employees make cheese three to four days a week, then sell it at local farmers' markets on the weekends, as well as supplying a variety of cheeses to chefs and retailers as far south as Seattle. While consumers can still be skeptical about goat cheese, Rhonda is a good saleswoman. "I tell people—you can't make a good product out of bad milk. I'm really pleased with my milk, it's good, sweet, and clean." More often than not, those people are immediate converts to the joys of Gothberg's exceptional farmstead cheeses.

19. GRACE HARBOR FARMS

TIM AND GRACE LUKENS

2347 Birch Bay Lynden Rd.

Custer, WA 98240

360-366-4151

graceharborfarms.com

GOAT'S MILK

STYLES OF CHEESE

Fresh

Chèvre

Yogurt

Aged

Gouda

Also sells bottled milk as well as goat's milk lotions and soaps

Tim Lukens specializes in making fresh chévre

Tim and Grace Lukens used to run an area bed-and-breakfast; their experience providing hospitality for visiting guests are evident at Grace Harbor Farms. The farm is decidedly visitor friendly, and the Lukenses encourage tourists to stop by, pet some goats, and sample the whole range of their goat's milk products.

The Lukenses initially got into cheese by way of their line of goat's milk soap and lotion products. But

Freshly made chévre hanging in cloth bags to drain

the goats came first—a vestige of their concern about Y2K. Tim laughs about that now, but as it turns out the goats have been the key to a thriving business. Tim and Grace started out making goat's milk soap and selling it at the Bellingham Farmers Market. Consumers responded to the soap and later to the lotions Grace developed, and the Lukenses found that they'd tapped a niche market of healing products

for people with skin allergies. Eventually they decided to diversify their operation by developing a cheese and goat's milk line in 2003.

Currently most of Grace Harbor Farms' milk goes out the door as bottled milk, but Tim is ramping up cheese production slowly after a brief hiatus. He's also tinkering with a cream separator and has plans to develop goat's milk ice cream, something that's sure to be a hit with visitors to the farm.

20. PLEASANT VALLEY DAIRY

JOYCE AND BARRY SNOOK

6804 Kickerville Rd.

Ferndale, WA 98248

360-366-5398

COW'S MILK

STYLES OF CHEESE

Aged

Farmstead

Gouda, plain and flavored/smoked

Mutschli

Nokkelost

George Train purchased 80 acres of farmland in Northwest Washington near Birch Bay in 1963. Even back in those days, making a go at farming was a difficult endeavor, so Train was forced to find work at the nearby aluminum-processing plant to support his family. He even put the farm up for sale for a time. When Train later went to France on business, he noticed what farmers there were doing with artisan cheese and came back with the idea of giving farmstead cheesemaking a try.

Pleasant Valley Farm exists today because the farm did not sell and necessity led Train down the cheesemaking path. He started with six cows, selling raw milk and developing a cheese business slowly over time. Gouda was a logical choice because of the relative simplicity of the process and equipment involved. He later developed one of Pleasant Valley's other varieties, Farmstead, in collaboration with Margaret Morris of Glengarry Cheesemaking Supply. Now retired, George lives with his wife, Dolores, in a house on a back corner of the farm, while Joyce Snook, George's daughter and now owner of Pleasant Valley with her husband, Barry, have taken over the business. Daughter Mattie is the family's third-generation cheesemaker, while son Seth manages the herd and milking duties.

Pleasant Valley has made all raw milk cheeses continuously since

Pleasant Valley Dairy has been making farmstead cheeses since the 1970s

the beginning. Their current herd of 75 cows, a mixed herd with Brown Swiss, Guernsey, Milking Shorthorn, Jersey, and others, delivers a blend of milk components perfect for cheesemaking. Joyce says the primary focus these days is maintaining the hard earned balance of factors, some tangible and some intangible, that has enabled the family to produce outstanding cheese for over three decades.

21. SAMISH BAY CHEESE COMPANY

SUZANNE AND ROGER WECHSLER

15115 Bow Hill Rd.

Bow, WA 98232

360-766-6707

samishbaycheese.com

COW'S MILK, CERTIFIED ORGANIC

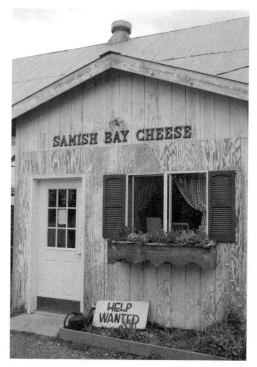

Visitors to the Skagit Valley are welcome to stop by the farm and purchase cheese from its shop

STYLES OF CHEESE

Fresh

Cheese curds

Farmer's cheese, plain and flavored

Feta

Mozzarella

Queso Fresco

Yogurt

Aged

Gouda, plain and flavored

Montasio

Mont Blanchard, plain and flavored

Port Edison

Suzanne and Roger Wechsler have been farming and making cheese at Rootabaga Country Farm since 1999. The farm's name is derived from Carl Sandburg's children's book *Rootabaga Stories*, which chronicles the main characters' travels to the fanciful Rootabaga country. The 150-acre farm is a diverse

All of Samish Bay's cow's milk cheeses are certified organic

venture, supporting a cheese-making operation as well as selling organic beef and pork raised on the farm.

The Wechslers make cheese from their herd of about 30 cows, a mixed bunch of Jerseys, Milking Short-horns, and other breeds that graze on the farm's verdant valley pasture most of the year. Their rich milk goes into the creamery's cheeses, which include Gouda (available both plain and flavored), Italian Style Montasio, and Port Edison, a softer but piquant cheese. Most recently, the Wechslers have expanded their range of offerings to include a line of fresh cheeses, including fresh mozzarella and farmer's cheese, as well as whole milk and cream-top yogurt.

22. SILVER SPRINGS CREAMERY

ERIC SUNDSTROM

256 East Hemmi Rd.

Lynden, WA 98264

360-820-1384

silverspringscreamery.com

COW'S MILK

STYLES OF CHEESE

Gouda

Jeddar *(cheddar made with Jersey cows' milk)*

Also sells ice cream, sorbet, and bottled milk

After a career in the dairy industry, Washington native Eric Sundstrom purchased a farm in Lynden, near Bellingham, in 2004. In a gorgeous valley with a view of Mt. Adams, his 40 acres include two small creeks that run through the property where salmon still return to spawn. It's picture-perfect pasture of the kind that's a key component in producing great milk for great cheese.

Sundstrom was licensed in 2006 to make cheese from the milk of his small herd of Jersey cows but suffered a setback in early 2007, when the farm's more than 100-year-old barn was destroyed in a fire. Since then he's been hard at work rebuilding and upgrading his cheesemaking facility, with an eye to be back up and running at full speed soon. Plans include an on-site shop with a view of the cheesemaking room, and Sundstrom hopes to focus on drawing visitors to his farm with ice cream as well as cheese.

CENTRAL/EASTERN WASHINGTON

23. ALPINE LAKES SHEEP CHEESE

CATHA AND ERIC LINK

PO Box 122

Leavenworth, WA 98826

509-548-5786

alpinelakescheese.com

SHEEP'S MILK

Creamy Bleu

Eric and Catha Link

STYLES OF CHEESE

Soft-Ripened

Camembert

Creamy Bleu

Aged

Mountain Tomme

Catha Link acquired her love for farming and dairy early in life. "I grew up in Vermont, back when the state still had a lot of small dairies," she remembers. "When we were young, my sister and I would hang out with the cows all day long." Later on her cheesemaking journey, she passed through a pear orchard. Catha and husband, Eric, acquired a farm in the Cascade Foothills near Leavenworth,

Alpine Lakes' dairy sheep and lambs

Washington, that included 4 acres of pear trees that hadn't been attended to for years. "We wanted to find something that could graze in the orchard without destroying the trees," says Catha. Cows and goats were out of the question, so the family settled on sheep as the ideal solution. Now the Links have a milking herd of about 25 East Friesian and Lacaune sheep that are happy to mow and digest the orchard grass—and the pear trees are doing just fine.

Catha began by experimenting with making cheese, yogurt, and other products from sheep's milk for several years, to the delight of friends and neighbors. "We wanted to eat healthy, wholesome food that we made ourselves, and liked to eat," she says. She also traveled back to Vermont, visiting several cheesemakers, including Vermont Shepherd, to understand more about the finer points of the cheeesemaking process. Alpine Lakes Sheep Cheese became officially licensed to make and sell cheese in December of 2006, and now they're selling out of their outstanding raw-milk cheeses.

24. LARKHAVEN FARM

M. CLARE PARIS AND SAM HOWELL

63 Yarnell Rd.

Tonasket, WA 98855

509-486-1199

larkhavenfarm.com

GOAT AND SHEEP'S MILK

STYLES OF CHEESE

Fresh
Whitestone Feta

Soft-Ripened
Rosa Rugosa *(sheep and goat's milk blend)*

Aged
Cayuse Mountain Goat
Shepherd's Gem

Cheesemaker M. Clare Paris is a Western Washington native who has lived in Tonasket since the early 1980s. For Clare and husband Sam Howell, developing a sustainable and healthy lifestyle for their family has long been high on their priority list.

Having kids changed Clare's life in a lot of ways, but particularly in relation to food. "It really radicalized me in terms of food sources," she says. "I also started to feel burdened by the amount of packaging I was picking up every time I shopped, so producing more and more of our own food was just a natural development." She bought her first goat from a friend and started using the milk to make cheese for her family. "For awhile, my goal was just to make cheese for my family, and for Christmas presents," she remembers.

Clare experimented with recipes from Ricki Carroll's *Home Cheese Making* book and worked to refine her own styles over several years. She also received a lot of support from esteemed Washington cheesemaker Sally Jackson, who lives a few miles up the road. "Sally was really encouraging," says Clare. "She told me, 'I don't know why more people don't do what I do.' That made it all seem so possible."

A lamb enjoys the summer sun at Larkhaven Farm

25. Monteillet Fromagerie

Joan and Pierre-Louis Monteillet

109 Ward Rd.

Dayton, WA 99328

509-382-1917

monteilletcheese.com

GOAT AND SHEEP'S MILK

VISITORS

*By appointment;
see Web site for
information about on-farm
lodging options*

STYLES OF CHEESE

Fresh

Fresh Chèvre, plain and flavored
Provencal (*marinated in olive oil and herbs*)

Soft-Ripened

Larzac
LeRoi
Mejean and Mejean Rouge (*marinated in wine*)
Perail (*sheep's milk*)

Aged

Causse Noir
Sauveterre

Visitors to Monteillet Fromagerie will enjoy the elegant and well-appointed tasting room

Joan, the farm girl from Eastern Washington, and Pierre-Louis, the Frenchman, first met when both were traveling in Oaxaca, Mexico. After several years of globe-trotting, the self-described hippies settled down in Southeastern Washington's Palouse region, running Joan's family's 2,000-acre wheat farm. Eventually they transitioned to a smaller and significantly more manageable

The Monteillets farm 30 acres of land next to the Touchet River near Walla Walla

30-acre farm in Dayton, Washington, along the Touchet River.

After spending time in France learning cheesemaking techniques (Pierre-Louis is originally from Millau, near Roquefort), they returned to develop their own cheeses made from the milk of the farm's sheep and goats. The Monteillets became the first artisan cheesemakers in the Walla Walla Valley when they started the fromagerie in 2002. Today the Monteillets and their luscious cheeses are a familiar, friendly presence at farmers' markets in Seattle and Portland.

26. PINE STUMP FARMS

CAREY HUNTER AND ALBERT ROBERTS

PO Box 1967

Omak, WA 98841

509-826-9492

pinestumpfarms.com

GOAT'S MILK

STYLES OF CHEESE

Aged

Asiago

French-style Crottin

Havarti

Parmesan

Romano

VISITORS

See their Web site for information about a variety of activities offered on the farm.

Pine Stump Farms specializes in aged goat's milk cheeses

Washington native Carey Hunter began her cheesemaking journey as many do, on a search for fresh, wholesome milk for her kids. "Then the kids grew up and we had extra milk," she laughs. That's when she started experimenting with other uses for the milk, making yogurt and kefir and fresh cheeses. Eventually, she looked for ways to not just use the milk but preserve it—and cheese was a natural solution to that dilemma. Even so, Carey firmly believes that cheesemaking is an art rooted in its surroundings. "I probably wouldn't be making cheese if it didn't want to happen here," she says.

Over time the cheese hobby became more serious, and in 2006 Pine Stump Farms became an officially licensed cheesemaking operation. But the story of Pine Stump Farms is not just about cheese—it's more that cheese is part of the story of Pine Stump Farms. It's what Carey calls their "integrated approach to land stewardship," a philosophy geared toward minimizing their footprint on the Earth. Caring for their land, located on the Confederated Tribes of the Colville Indian Reservation, is a project that both Carey and partner Albert take very seriously; their commitment is reflected in their efforts to educate the community about sustainability and resource management issues.

Carey Hunter and Albert Roberts are passionate about careful, responsible land and animal management

27. QUESERIA BENDITA

BENEDITA AGUILAR MONTES AND SANDRA AGUILAR

512 S Third St.

Yakima, WA 98901

509-574-8587

COW'S MILK

STYLES OF CHEESE

Fresh

Panela

Queso Fresco

Requeson

When Benedita Aguilar was 10 years old, her father bought a cow for the family ranch in Michoacan, Mexico. She learned to milk the cow and made cheese from the cow's milk with her mother. Today she continues the cheesemaking tradition at Queseria Bendita ("Blessed Cheese") in Yakima, Washington.

Like many cheesemakers, Benedita never lost her passion for cheesemaking once she acquired it. Over the years she continued to make cheese for friends and family, becoming known for the quality and taste of her cheese. "People would ask me all the time—why don't you sell this?" she says (as translated by daughter Sandra). Queseria Bendita started as a formal business in 2000 and has flourished ever since.

Queseria Bendita started making cheese with 200 gallons of milk per week and they have since expanded considerably. Today the operation uses a 500-gallon pasteurizer, a bulk tank, open

vats, and considerable equipment associated with cheesemaking. Benedita, daughter Sandra, and three other employees process 2,000 gallons of milk weekly, purchased from the nearby Dairgold milk processing plant in Sunnyside. Then Sandra drives the packaged fresh cheeses to their various distribution points in Washington and Oregon later in the week. Come Monday, the process starts all over again.

28. QUILLISASCUT CHEESE COMPANY

RICK AND LORA LEA MISTERLY

2409 Pleasant Valley Rd

Rice, WA 99167

509-738-2011

quillisascut.com

GOAT'S MILK

VISITORS

*By appointment;
check Web site for
class schedule*

STYLES OF CHEESE

Aged

Ash Tomme

Curado, plain and flavored

UFO

Viejo

*A trio of Quillisascut's cheeses—left to right:
Curado, Curado with lavender, and UFO*

Rick and Lora Lea Misterly are among the first wave of artisan cheesemakers in the Pacific Northwest; they've been making cheese in Rice, Washington (northwest of Spokane), since 1987. More than 20 years later, they're amazed to find themselves artisan cheesemaking veterans.

Rick, originally from Southern California, settled in nearby Republic, Washington, in the 1970s. He later met Lora Lea, a native of Leavenworth, Washington, and they purchased 26 acres in 1980, later expanding by 10 acres when nearby land became available. The farm is nestled into the Huckleberry Mountains near Rice, Washington,

Veteran cheesemakers Lora Lea and Rick Misterly are pioneers of farm-based educational practices

northwest of Spokane; namesake Quillisascut Creek flows through the property. As the apocryphal tale goes, the name means "place of scattered bushes," a reference to a time when Native Americans would burn off vegetation to encourage the growth of low brush in the area.

Over the years, the Misterlys have raised sheep, turkeys, cows, and a variety of other livestock, but cheese has been one constant, made from the milk of their current herd of about 60 goats. The Misterlys still hand milk every goat, with the milk going right into their line of raw milk cheeses. Lora Lea's mother made her own cheeses at home when Lora Lea was growing up, including cottage cheese, farmer's cheese, and pot cheese, sort of a variation on cottage cheese. When Lora Lea set out to make cheese herself, she happened to come across a recipe for Manchego, which worked well with the flavor profile of the farm's goats' milk; that cheese became the Curado that she still makes today.

The farm continues to evolve. In 2002 the Misterlys started a thriving farm school that attracts people from all over the region; they stay at the farm, learn about sustainable food production, and develop meals around meat and produce from the farm. *Chefs on the Farm: Recipes and Inspiration from the Quillisascut Farm School of the Domestic Arts* by Lora Lea Misterly and Shannon Borg, a book chronicling the Quillisascut Farm experience with seasonal recipes, was released in the fall of 2008.

29. SALLY JACKSON CHEESES

SALLY AND ROGER JACKSON

16 Nealy Rd.

Oroville, WA 98844

509-485-3722

sallyjacksoncheeses.com

COW, GOAT, AND SHEEP'S MILK

STYLES OF CHEESE

Aged

Cow, goat, and sheep's milk cheeses wrapped in grape and chestnut leaves.

Sally Jackson chooses from an assortment of her wares

Sally and Roger Jackson moved to rural Eastern Washington from New York City in the 1970s (Roger is originally from Ellensburg, Washington). They bought land in the Okanogan Valley near the Canadian border and started a subsistence farm. After securing a government grant to start a cheese plant, Sally Jackson was licensed to make cheese in 1979.

Starting out was an adventure. "I made everything—butter, cottage cheese, and even ice cream," she remembers. Among Jackson's first customers were the members of a nearby commune; tiny Okanogan River Co-op in Tonasket became one of her first retail outlets. Many Seattle chefs and retail merchants remember Sally and Roger's old Volvo and the cheese treasures carefully bundled within.

Over time, Sally developed a local, then national reputation for her distinctive cheeses. Though she has made a variety of styles of cheese over the years from fresh chèvre to mountain-style tommes, today she focuses on making her signature 2–3 pound wheels of cheese

Jackson has developed a national reputation for her gorgeous leaf-wrapped cheeses

wrapped in local chestnut and grape leaves Her limited supply is in great demand nationwide.

The Jackson farm is rustic and remote, both by choice; for years Sally and Roger Jackson lived without electricity, farming and raising three children. Though they now have both electricity and a telephone, Sally continues to make her cheeses using a wood stove in her cheese plant in a manner resembling an Old World master. Years of experience tell her when the curds are ready by touch; she then scoops the curds into ceramic molds made by a local artist. The cheeses are salted and wrapped in leaves, then aged typically three to four months.

Sally Jackson is a pioneer in the Northwest artisan cheesemaking industry, singlehandedly developing a market for artisan cheese in Washington at a time when today's ubiquitous farmers' markets and local, sustainable food trends were unheard of. In addition to making cheese, Jackson regularly dispenses advice to local goat and sheep keepers and has mentored numerous Washington cheesemakers over the years, including M. Clare Paris of Larkhaven Farm, Kelli Estrella of Estrella Family Creamery, and Catha Link of Alpine Lakes Sheep Cheese. Several years ago she traveled to Bangladesh, teaching cheesemaking to impoverished communities.

30. WASHINGTON STATE UNIVERSITY CREAMERY

RUSS SALVADALENA, CREAMERY MANAGER

PO Box 641122

Pullman, WA 99164

800-457-5442

wsu.edu/creamery

COW'S MILK

STYLES OF CHEESE

Aged

American Cheddar, plain and smoked

Cougar Gold

Crimson Fire

Viking, plain or flavored

One of only a few university operated creameries left in the United States, Washington State University Creamery started as a third-party operation in the early 1900s which provided milk to the university's dining hall. The university took over the creamery in 1948, and eventually developed a cheesemaking operation as a means to use excess milk. The creamery was primarily a fluid milk operation until the 1970s, when it began to make and market cheese in earnest.

Many consumers know Washington State University cheeses by their distinctive packaging—they come in tin cans. The can concept evolved during the 1940s, when Washington State University conducted research, in cooperation with the federal government and American Can Company, into cheese storage options. While the research was in some sense less than successful, as canning alone could not preserve cheese for long periods (it still needs to

All of Washington State University's cheeses are packaged in signature tin cans

be refrigerated), Washington State University's signature packaging is used for all of the creamery's cheeses today.

Cougar Gold, the university's best-selling cheese, was developed during those early canning experiments. The cultures used to make the cheese were specifically formulated to minimize expressed gasses that could cause the can to explode. Consumers loved the cheese, and the university still maintains the original cultures developed by Dr. Golding and uses them to make Cougar Gold. The creamery currently produces over 200,000 cans of cheese per year, including Cougar Gold and other products like traditional cheddar and Jack cheeses.

Washington State University Creamery is a self-supporting, education-focused operation that is part of the university's Food Science department. Students work in all phases of the operation, from making cheese and ice cream, working in Ferdinand's, the retail store, to working in the inventory and packaging facility. Even the milk comes from a university-owned herd of Holstein cows cared for by students from the Animal Science Department.

Washington State University has also has contributed significantly to the development of the artisan cheesemaking industry in the Pacific Northwest over the past several decades through its education programs and extension services. Numerous Northwest cheesemakers, including Sandra Aguilar (Queseria Bendita), Will O'Donnell (Mt. Townsend Creamery), and David Wood (Salt Spring Island Cheese Company) honed their skills by attending one or more of the university creamery's courses.

New in Central/Eastern Washington

31. Sunny Pine Farm

Ed and Vicky Welch
932A Twisp River Rd.
Twisp, WA 98825
509-997-4811
sunnypinefarm.com

Ed and Vicky Welch have been farming near Twisp, Washington, in the Methow Valley since the 1970s. They ran an organic produce operation for many years (they still grow lavender for making essential oils) but more recently they phased out large-scale vegetable farming in favor of a goat dairy and cheesemaking operation. Sunny Pine is currently making fresh chèvre and feta, both plain and flavored, and goat's-milk yogurt; Vicky says that it's all they can do to keep up with demand. Sunny Pine Farm's cheese is also the first certified organic goat cheese in Washington.

CHAPTER 3

IDAHO

1. BALLARD FAMILY DAIRY AND CHEESE

STEVE AND STACIE BALLARD

1764 S 2100 E

Gooding, ID 83330

208-934-4972

ballardcheese.com

COW'S MILK

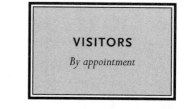

VISITORS

By appointment

STYLES OF CHEESE

Fresh

Cheese curds

Feta

Golden Greek Halloumi

Ricotta

Aged

Cheddar, plain and with hot peppers

Danish Pearl

Idaho Jersey Gem

Idaho White Cheddar

Travis Ballard hard at work on a batch of cheddar

Californians Steve and Stacie Ballard didn't move to the small town of Gooding, Idaho (about an hour and a half southeast of Boise), out of the blue. Steve's family lives in the area and he grew up spending summers there. So when the former diesel mechanic decided he'd had enough of his job, he knew he wanted to start a farm in Gooding. Stacie, a former waitress originally from Long Beach, had never lived in the country. "I'd never even had a pet!" she

laughs. Now she has 70 doe-eyed Jersey cows that keep her company.

The Ballards made the move in the mid-1990s and started a 50-acre dairy farm. After selling milk to a local processor for several years, the Ballards (like many dairy farmers) found that it was going to be difficult, if not impossible, to sustain a dairy farm long term. They decided to innovate, attending several cheesemaking courses, including programs at Cal State San Luis Obispo and Washington State University, in order to get themselves up to speed. By 2004 they'd built a cheese plant, and in the process they also became Idaho's only producer of farmstead cow's milk cheeses.

While Gooding, Idaho, is known primarily for its industrial cheese production (the nearby Glanbia plant is reportedly one of the largest in the world), the Ballards are decidedly the opposite—small, artisan, and farmstead. Making cheese is an all-around family operation: son Travis is in charge of cheese; dad Steve concentrates on the herd; and mom Stacie manages the business side. Several part-time employees also pitch in and everyone lends a hand when it's time to mill the curds or salt the pressed cheeses. Demand has grown steadily for their products—their Golden Greek Halloumi, in particular, has been a big success with local consumers and restaurants. The Ballards are busy making their mark in the world of Idaho artisan cheesemaking.

2. LITEHOUSE BLEU CHEESE FACTORY

125 S. 2nd Ave
Sandpoint, Idaho 83864
208-263-2030
litehousefoods.com

VISITORS
10 AM–6 PM, Mon–Sat
Closed Sundays

STYLES OF CHEESE

Blue Cheese
Idaho Bleu Cheese Crumbles
Heart of Idaho Bleu Cheese
Monarch Mountain Gorgonzola Crumbles

Visitors to the factory can watch blue cheese being made

Litehouse Foods is best known for the salad dressings (including several "bleu" cheese varieties) it has been making since the 1960s. For many years, Litehouse purchased the cheese used in its dressing products. In 2001, the company brought the cheese production in-house, hiring veteran cheesemaker Ralph Stuart to run the operation. Today this little cheese plant in the heart of downtown Sandpoint, Idaho (otherwise best known as a ski town), produces about 1 million pounds of blue cheese per year. Much of the cheese goes into Litehouse dressings, but the company also sells several standalone cheese products,

Litehouse—the little cheese plant in the heart of ski country

including the newly developed Monarch Mountain Gorgonzola Crumbles.

The Sandpoint factory is small but full of activity; visitors are welcome and can view the operation from the windowed viewing area that runs alongside the vats. A collection of photos documents every step of the operation, from milk to pressing to piercing to packaging. In addition to the self-guided tour, visitors may also sample and purchase Litehouse products and other locally made foods and crafts in the factory store.

3. ROLLINGSTONE CHÈVRE

CHUCK AND KAREN EVANS

PO Box 683

Parma, Idaho 83660

208-722-6460

homepage.mac.com/chevre

GOAT'S MILK

STYLES OF CHEESE

Fresh

Fresh Chèvres and Tortas, plain and flavored

Fromage Blanc de Parma

Soft-Ripened

Bleu Agé

Aged

Brandywine

Idaho Goatster

Late Harvest Wheel

Waxed Wheels: Anise/Lavender and Orange Zest Pecan

Chuck Evans grew up on the same farm where he and his wife, Karen, now operate Rolling-stone Chèvre

Chuck and Karen Evans established Idaho's first goat dairy in 1988, then one of only a few goat dairies in the Pacific Northwest. Twenty years later, while goat's milk cheesemakers have multiplied elsewhere in the region, Rollingstone Chèvre remains the sole representative in Idaho.

Chuck and Karen first started keeping goats while living in the small town of Rollingstone, Minnesota, when they found that their daughter was allergic to cow's milk. Chuck, then an art professor, tended to the goats in his spare time. Eventually Karen, an accomplished artist, started experimenting with making cheese from the milk. In 1980, Chuck left academia and the family moved to Parma, Idaho, to the farm where Chuck grew up. With ample encouragement from friends and a local food critic, says Karen, selling cheese began to seem like a real possibility. Cheesemaking was also a practical

Some of Rollingstone's purebred Saanen goats

alternative to the daunting prospect of marketing and selling her art in rural Southern Idaho.

Though it's tempting to think that a town called Parma might have some association with the Italian cheesemaking town of the same name, in fact Parma, Idaho, is not (nor was it ever) a small Italian enclave. Instead, Chuck and Karen have singlehandedly forged their own cheesemaking tradition. Their outstanding European-style fresh chèvres, tortes, and aged cheeses have developed a national following. Considering the thriving cheese business they've developed, it's amazing that they still manage to make art in their scarce spare time.

CHAPTER 4

BRITISH COLUMBIA

Vancouver Area / Fraser Valley

Vancouver Island / Gulf Islands

Thompson Okanagan / Kootenays

VANCOUVER AREA/ FRASER VALLEY

1. THE FARM HOUSE NATURAL CHEESES

DEBRA AMREIN-BOYES

5634 McCallum Rd.

Agassiz, BC V0M 1A1

604-796-8741

farmhousecheeses.com

COW AND GOAT'S MILK, PROVINCIALLY REGISTERED

VISITORS

*Farm Store open
Monday–Saturday,
10 AM–5 PM; Sunday 1–5 PM
Closed holidays and the first
three weeks of January*

STYLES OF CHEESE

Fresh

Fromage Frais
Cheese Curds
Quark
Feta

Soft-ripened

Brie *(goat and cow's milk versions)*
Farm House Camembert
La Pyramide *(goat's milk)*
La Florette *(goat's milk)*
St. George *(goat's milk)*

Aged

Cheddar *(goat and cow's milk versions)*
Gruyere
Country Morning *(cow's milk)*
Goat Caerphilly
Gouda *(goat and cow's milk versions)*

Blue

Castle Blue

Washed-rind

Alpine Gold

Also sells goat's milk and butter

Some styles of cheese must be aged to reach their maximum flavor potential

*W*ith dairy farms disappearing all across British Columbia, Fraser Valley dairy farmers George Boyes and Debra Amrein-Boyes made a decision to transform their cow's milk dairy by adding a cheesemaking operation. "Agriculture is a difficult world to survive in," says Debra. "You either have to expand your operation or diversify to survive. We chose to diversify." Though area farmers viewed their move with considerable skepticism, The Farm House Natural Cheeses began selling its first handmade farmstead cheeses in 2004.

George grew up on a dairy farm in England and has a diploma from the Royal Agricultural College. He's owned and managed this Agassiz dairy for over 20 years. Debra, a native of Saskatchewan, grew up on a farm as well, but one devoted to growing grain and raising beef cattle rather than dairying. She later lived in Switzerland for 10 years in an Alpine farming village, where she learned to make soft cheeses. "Dairying and cheesemaking are a part of life up there," she remembers. "Every year you've got the cows going up to the Alps to graze in the summer and they come back down with headdresses on, it's a big festival."

Today George runs the dairy operation while Debra manages the cheesemaking side using milk from the herd of Holstein, Guernsey, and Brown Swiss cows. More recently, goats joined the farm, says Debra, because of growing demand for goat's milk cheeses. With the help of several employees, she has developed a range of cow and goat's milk cheeses, from soft-ripened brie to cheddars to blues. "This allows me to be creative," says

105

Debra, and the variety also means that there's likely at least one type of cheese that everyone will enjoy.

The Farm House has become a vital part of a lively agritourism industry in the Agassiz area. The on-farm shop welcomes visitors and sells all of their cheeses as well as gelato and other locally made products and gifts. After five years in business, Amrein-Boyes can say for certain that cheese has indeed transformed this dairy. "It has answered our need for agricultural viability but also fulfilled the increasing demand for quality food from local farms."

The Farm House welcomes visitors to their on-site shop, where they sell locally made foods and crafts as well as cheese

2. GOAT'S PRIDE DAIRY AT McLENNAN CREEK

DYKSTRA FAMILY

30854 Olund Rd.

Abbotsford, BC V4X 1Z9

604-854-6261 or 855-610-1004

goatspride.com

GOAT'S MILK, CERTIFIED ORGANIC, PROVINCIALLY REGISTERED

STYLES OF CHEESE

Fresh

Fresh Chèvre

Feta

Yogurt

Soft-ripened

Blue Caprina

Chevrotina

Aged

Caprabella

Capramonte *(plain and smoked)*

Tomme de Chèvre

Gouda

Blue

Blue Capri

Also sells goat's milk

Founders Jill Tyndale and Chris Watkiss started the original incarnation of McLennan Creek Goat Dairy when they discovered that one of their sons was allergic to cow's milk. In time they built a herd. "The goats started out as a hobby, but then we started looking for ways to make them pay for themselves," says Chris. Initially they sold fluid milk to a local processor and later began making cheese.

Along the way, Tyndale and Watkiss hired Jason Dykstra as a

Salmon still return annually to spawn in McLennan Creek, which runs through the dairy's property

part-time cheesemaker. Jason, who had been in their 4-H club as a youngster, was already familiar with goats since his family had operated Goat's Pride Dairy in the Fraser Valley for years. Later, when they began to contemplate selling, the solution was right in front of them. In 2006, the Dykstra family purchased the operation and began cheese production at the McLennan Creek location—same cheeses, same cheesemaker, new name.

While Jason is a graphic artist by training (he designed the farm's new logo), today he's making cheese full time—make that more than full time.

He's been doing it long enough now that he's as adept at planning his production schedule as he is at making cheese. Family members pitch in with animal care and milking the more than 120 goats; Goat's Pride also supplements their supply with additional milk from local goat farms.

3. RIDGECREST DAIRY LTD.

DAVE VERDONK

Box 10 – 32929 Mission Way

Mission, BC V2V 6E4

604-820-4001

ridgecrestdairies.com

COW'S MILK, PROVINCIALLY REGISTERED

STYLES OF CHEESE

Fresh

Panir

Neufchatel

Yogurt

Aged

Cheddar

Gouda

Dave Verdonk grew up on a dairy farm in the Fraser Valley. His father, a dairy chemist, started out in the 1980s selling whole milk to restaurants, which used it to make their own cheese. Eventually, the local Punjabi Business Association approached the family about making panir cheese, since cheesemaking was a time- and space-intensive process for restaurants. At the time, says Verdonk, no other companies were making panir in British Columbia. Panir soon became Ridgecrest Dairy's mainstay, though today they also produce several styles of aged cheese and a whole milk yogurt. Dave says he's currently working on perfecting what he calls "cheese jerky," a smoked cheese product.

4. SCARDILLO CHEESE COMPANY

ROCKY AND KATHY SCARDILLO

7865 Venture St.

Burnaby, BC V5A 1V1

604-420-9892

COW'S MILK, FEDERALLY REGISTERED

Scardillo

STYLES OF CHEESE

ITALIAN SPECIALTIES INCLUDE:

Fresh

Bocconcini

Trecce

Aged

Caciocavallo

Scamorza

Toma

Burini

Paolo and Maria Scardillo emigrated to British Columbia in 1959 from Tricarico, Matera, in Southern Italy. These former sheep farmers started out making Italian-style cheeses at a cow's milk dairy in Richmond, near Vancouver. The substantial Italian immigrant population in the Vancouver area at the time provided an instant customer base. "My parents would make cheese in the morning," says son Rocky, who now runs the company, "and then sell it directly to the all of the small Italian delis in the afternoon." The Scardillos later rented space from Avalon Dairy in Vancouver and eventually the operation grew and moved to suburban Burnaby, where it is today.

Scardillo Cheese has grown considerably from its humble beginnings into a sizeable cheesemaking operation today. Over the years, they've expanded their offerings to include additional styles of cheese such as cheddar and queso fresco as well the traditional Italian specialties. Rocky and wife Kathy's sons, Paolo and Anthony, are currently working in the family business, the third generation of Scardillos to carry on the family cheesemaking tradition.

VANCOUVER ISLAND/ GULF ISLANDS

5. HILARY'S ARTISAN CHEESE

HILARY AND PATTY ABBOTT

1737 Cowichan Bay Rd.

Cowichan Bay, BC V0R 1N1

888-480-7600

hilaryscheese.com

COW AND GOAT'S MILK, PROVINCIALLY REGISTERED

VISITORS

Cheese Shop and Deli open
9 AM–5 PM every day;
closed Monday and Tuesday
during the off-season.

STYLES OF CHEESE

Fresh
Chèvre
Quark

Soft-ripened
St. Clair
St. Michel *(goat's milk)*

Aged
Belle Ann *(goat's milk)*
Cowichan Blue
Goat Cheddar
Red Dawn
Sacre Blue *(goat's milk)*
St. Denis
Valley Blue *(goat's milk)*
Yoo Boo Blue

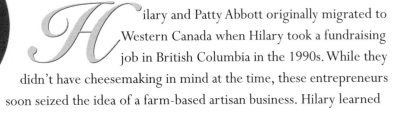

Hilary and Patty Abbott originally migrated to Western Canada when Hilary took a fundraising job in British Columbia in the 1990s. While they didn't have cheesemaking in mind at the time, these entrepreneurs soon seized the idea of a farm-based artisan business. Hilary learned

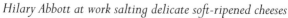
Hilary Abbott at work salting delicate soft-ripened cheeses

the craft of cheesemaking by taking the Washington State University cheesemaking course as well as through time and experience. Today he employs several assistants who help him in making over a dozen European-style goat and cow's milk cheeses. Patty, a former banker, runs the business side of the operation while Hilary manages the cheesemaking.

While many artisan cheesemakers sell their cheeses at farm shops, the Abbotts (both of whom came to cheeesemaking from the business world) have taken the idea one step farther. In 2007 they opened a shop called Hilary's Cheese and Deli in nearby Cowichan Bay, which sells a variety of European cheeses as well as Hilary's own line. "We have a great market for cheese in British Columbia," says Hilary, "it's a very international population and has two large urban centers in Vancouver and Victoria." The Abbotts aim to capitalize on this potential by opening several more Hilary's Cheese & Deli outposts in British Columbia in the future.

6. LITTLE QUALICUM CHEESEWORKS

CLARKE AND NANCY GOURLAY

403 Lowry's Rd.

Parksville, BC V9P 2B5

250-954-3931 or 877-248-4353

cheeseworks.ca

COW'S MILK, PROVINCIALLY REGISTERED

VISITORS

Farm open

Monday–Saturday,

9 AM–5 PM

STYLES OF CHEESE

Fresh

Cheese Curds

Fromage Frais

Feta

Soft-ripened

Island Bries

San Pareil

Aged

Caerphilly

Monterey Jill

Qualicum Spice

Raclette

Rathtrevor

*N*ancy and Clarke Gourlay spent several years overseas during the 1990s doing missionary work in Turkey, Afghanistan, and Switzerland. While in Switzerland, they found themselves immersed in a culture that revered cheesemaking. Later, when they returned to British Columbia, they decided to channel that inspiration into a life of farming and making cheese.

The Gourlays started Little Qualicum Cheeseworks in 2001. Nancy started out using her kitchen as a workshop, testing recipes and varieties until she found ones she liked. She also traveled back to Switzerland to learn from the source, and her Swiss-inspired cheeses

reflect these experiences. The Gourlays later moved to their current location at Morningstar Farm in Parksville, which they've developed into both a cheese-making operation and agritourism destination. The farm welcomes visitors and features an engaging self-guided tour that invites visitors to view all aspects of a working dairy operation, including the milking parlor, pastures, calf pens, and the cheesemaking facility. Visitors can also sample and purchase the entire line of Little Qualicum's farmstead cheeses from the soft-ripened and cleverly named Island Bries to the Swiss-style Rathtrevor and Raclette.

Little Qualicum is a popular tourist destination, offering self-guided farm tours and a well-stocked farm shop

7. MOONSTRUCK ORGANIC CHEESES

SUSAN AND JULIA GRACE

1306 Beddis Rd.

Salt Spring Island, BC V8K 2C9

250-537-4987

moonstruckcheese.com

COW'S MILK, CERTIFIED ORGANIC, PROVINCIALLY REGISTERED

Julia Grace is Moonstruck's cheesemaker; rich blue cheeses are her specialty

STYLES OF CHEESE

Soft-ripened

Ash-Ripened Camembert

Blue Moon

Savory Moon

White Moon

Aged

White Grace

Blue

Baby Blue

Beddis Blue

Blossom's Blue

Twenty years ago, Nova Scotia native Julia Grace was working for the Canadian government in Ottawa, Ontario. Her career has changed just a bit since those days—she's now making cheese on Salt Spring Island in British Columbia. Moonstruck Organic Cheese evolved in 1998 out of the certified organic produce operation Julia was running with partner Susan on the island. After Susan became interested in Jersey cows, the pair acquired one, and it soon became clear that

A few of Moonstruck's Jersey cows graze contentedly on Salt Spring Island

making cheese would be a more profitable endeavor than growing produce. Today the Graces milk a thriving herd of Jerseys that graze on their 30 acres overlooking Ganges Bay.

Julia honed her cheesemaking skills by practice and by talking to experienced cheesemakers. David Wood, who had started nearby Salt Spring Island Cheese Company a few years earlier, was also very helpful. "The truth of the matter," says Julia, "is that cheesemaking is not hard, consistent cheesemaking is what's hard." Even so, blue cheeses came easily and today Moonstruck's Blossom's Blue (named for a favorite cow) and Beddis Blue rank among the best blue cheeses made in the region.

The Graces have followed organic practices on their farm since the beginning. "I feel more comfortable being in this world doing things that way," Julia says. Having weathered the vagaries of the market, weather, and economy over the past decade, it's clear that Julia and Susan reap more than just money as a reward for their hard work. Julia sums it up this way: "There's not much lovelier under the sun than a contented Jersey cow."

Salt Spring Island Cheese Company's popular fresh chévre comes packaged in a myriad of delicious color-flavorings like bright green basil, a rainbow of edible flowers like nasturtiums and pansies, and red-hot chilies.

LEFT: *Rivers Edge Chévre Illahee Tomme is an aged raw milk goat cheese rubbed with truffle oil. The name comes from a Chinook word meaning "of the land."* ABOVE: *Pat Morford of Rivers Edge Chévre specializes in gorgeous soft-ripened cheeses that she and her daughters, Spring and Astraea, craft in logs, rounds, and pyramids. The beautiful Sunset Bay is made with a layer of smoked paprika running through the center in homage to a coastal sunset.*

ABOVE: *Tumalo Farms' popular Fenacho is a Gouda-style goat's milk cheese with the addition of the East Indian spice fenugreek. The unique flavoring delivers distinct butterscotch and maple notes and hints of spice.* RIGHT: *Kelli Estrella of Estrella Family Creamery makes a variety of aged raw milk cheeses like Guapier, a cow's milk Morbier-style cheese with a layer of vegetable ash running through the center (top of the stack).*

UPPER LEFT: *To make Rollingstone Chévre's Brandywine, Karen Evans ages chévre in brandy and cider then wraps the cheese in grape leaves in the style of a French Banon.*

BOTTOM RIGHT: *Beecher's Flagship Reserve is made in large wheels, or truckles, wrapped in cloth, and carefully nurtured during the one-year-plus aging process. The result is a British-style cheddar that placed first among aged cheddars and second overall in a field of over 1,200 cheeses at the 2007 American Cheese Society Competition.*

A Pacific Northwest classic, Rogue River Blue was developed by David Gremmels and Cary Bryant soon after they purchased Rogue Creamery in 2002.

A few of Fraga Farm's certified organic goat's milk cheeses: Rio Santiam (top), Aged Cheddar and Bandage Wrapped Cheddar (bottom).

8. NATURAL PASTURES CHEESE COMPANY

635 McPhee Ave.

Courtenay, BC V9N 2Z7

866-244-4422

naturalpastures.com

COW AND WATER BUFFALO MILK, FEDERALLY REGISTERED

VISITORS

*Shop open Janaunary–October,
1 PM–4 PM; November–December,
9 AM–4 PM. Closed the last
10 days of the year.*

STYLES OF CHEESE

Fresh

Cheese Curds

Mozzarella di Bufala

Soft-ripened

Comox Brie

Comox Camembert

Triple Cream Camembert

Aged

Amsterdammer

Boerenkaas

La Scala

Verdelait, plain and flavored

Edgar, Doug, and Phillip Smith are the third generation of caretakers on their family's 600-acre Beaver Meadows Farm in Vancouver Island's Comox Valley. When changes in the local dairy industry led them to consider alternative ways of marketing their milk supply, they started Natural Pastures Cheese Company in 2001.

Master cheesemaker Paul Sutter learned cheesemaking the Old World way, through the Swiss master cheesemaking program. He first traveled from his native Switzerland to British Columbia to work for fellow Swiss expatriates Hani and Theres Gasser, then owners of Mountain Meadow Sheep Dairy, in 1995. Sutter worked for several

other British Columbia cheesemakers over the next few years,
eventually finding his way to Vancouver Island and settling in as a
cheesemaker at Natural Pastures
Cheese Company just months
after it opened.

Sutter's background and
experience proved to be the
recipe for success for Natural
Pastures. Just months after he
started working at the company,
three of his cheeses (Comox
Brie, Boerenkaas, and Verdelait
with Cumin) were awarded Best

COURTESY NATURAL PASTURES CHEESE CO.

*Natural Pastures is the sole Canadian producer of Mozzarella di
Bufala, made from the milk of nearby Fairburn Farms' water buffalos*

in Category awards at the biannual Canadian Cheese Grand Prix competition, the only British
Columbian cheeses so honored. Most recently, Natural Pastures secured yet another First
Place for Comox Brie at the World Cheese Awards in Wisconsin in 2008.

9. SALT SPRING ISLAND CHEESE COMPANY

DAVID AND NANCY WOOD

285 Reynolds Rd.

Salt Spring Island, BC V8K 1Y2

250-653-2300

saltspringcheese.com

GOAT AND SHEEP'S MILK, FEDERALLY REGISTERED

STYLES OF CHEESE

Fresh

Feta

Fresh Chèvre, plain and flavored

Soft-ripened

Juliette

Aged

Montaña *(sheep's milk)*

VISITORS

*On-site farm shop open
11 AM–5 PM, daily,
May–September; 11 AM–4 PM
on weekends during the
rest of the year.*

Fresh chévre awaits packaging in the cheese room at Salt Spring Island Cheese Company

David Wood and his family left Toronto and the eponymous David Wood Food Shop for rural British Columbia and a slower lifestyle in 1990. Wood's first foray into cheesemaking came soon after when he began exploring the idea of making cheese from sheep's milk. "People thought it was a joke at the time when I said I was going to milk sheep. Nobody'd ever heard of someone milking them," says Wood. Seizing the opportunity to buy cheesemaking equipment from a defunct goat's milk cheesemaking operation on nearby Gabriola Island in the mid-

David Wood owned a specialty food shop in Toronto before starting Salt Spring Island Cheese Company

1990s, Salt Spring Island Cheese Company was officially up and running in the summer of 1996.

While sheep's milk was the initial inspiration, Wood says the business really hit its stride when he switched to making goat's milk cheeses. "We realized at the end of our first year that we needed a year-round milk supply." Goat's milk now makes up 90 percent of Salt Spring's cheese line, though they still make one aged sheep's milk cheese seasonally, the manchego-style Montaña.

After becoming federally registered in 2007, Salt Spring Island Cheese Company has expanded its distribution into the Toronto area, where the name David Wood is already associated with good food. While the business continues to grow, Wood is committed to maintaining high standards. "I want the consumer to feel that there's been a fair exchange when they buy our cheese, that it delivers on its promise," says Wood. With demand continuing to grow, Canadian consumers seem confident that Salt Spring Island cheese will indeed keep its promises.

handmade salt spring island goat cheese

A UNIQUE NORTHWEST DAIRY

10. FAIRBURN FARM WATER BUFFALO DAIRY

J. DARREL AND ANTHEA ARCHER

3330 Jackson Rd.

Duncan, BC V9L 6N7

250-746-4621

fairburnfarm.bc.ca

Darrel Archer

One of only a few significant milking herds in North America (the others are in California, Michigan and Vermont), the Fairburn Farm Water Buffalo live on a 130-acre farm nestled in the Cowichan Valley north of Victoria. Darrel Archer grew up on the historic farm, an old homestead that his parents purchased in 1945.

While searching for innovative ways to support the farm, Darrel's wife, Anthea, came across an article in a John Deere magazine that discussed these majestic creatures. "The article mentioned a dairy herd in North Devon, England," says Anthea. After doing some research, the Archers traveled to England to meet Robert Palmer, who'd been the first to bring water buffalo to England from Romania.

Politics almost ended the Archers' experiment. After they'd acquired

Water buffalo are gregarious, curious creatures

their first 19 buffalo from Bulgaria by way of Denmark, a mad cow scare in Denmark (affecting only one cow) caught the eye of Canadian regulatory authorities. A protracted legal battle ensued, but eventually the government forced the Archers to destroy the entire herd. They were allowed to keep the offspring born in Canada, however, and it is from these animals that their herd of 60 (about 30 currently milking) has grown.

Water buffalo are affectionate and curious. "They're not as aloof as cows can be," says Darrel, "they love to be petted." While the animals were a little skeptical about being milked at first, now they are very attached to their once-a-day schedule. "They don't want to leave the barn after the morning milking," says Anthea. "They like to have a little visit."

The Archers finally started milking in earnest in 2006. They currently sell all the herd's milk to Natural Pastures Cheese Company, which uses this rare commodity to make mozzarella di bufala by hand, once a week—the only authentic buffalo-milk mozzarella currently being made in Canada. Water buffalo milk is much higher in butterfat and protein than cow or goat's milk, making the resulting cheese richer and more flavorful. We're lucky to be able to enjoy this type of cheese made right here in the Pacific Northwest.

THOMPSON OKANAGAN/KOOTENAYS

11. CARMELIS GOAT CHEESE

OFRI AND OFER BARMOR

170 Timberline Rd.

Kelowna, BC V1W 4J6

250-870-3117

carmelisgoatcheese.com

GOAT'S MILK, FEDERALLYREGISTERED

VISITORS

Open March 1–April 30, 7 days a week, 11 AM–5 PM; May 1–October 15, 7 days a week, 10 AM–6 PM; October 16–December 31, Monday–Saturday, 11 AM–4 PM; closed January and February.

STYLES OF CHEESE

Fresh

Chèvre, plain and flavored

Feta

Labnae

Soft-ripened

Blue Velvet

Chabichu

Heavenly

Misty

Moonlight

Aged

Carmel

Goat Gruyere

Lior/ Lior Special Edition

Tuscany *(plain and smoked)*

Vintage

Blue

Goatgonzola

Fifteen years ago, Israeli sheep farmers Ofri and Ofer Barmor found themselves struggling with daughter Carmel's respiratory problems. Just as the couple was contemplating surgery to repair her damaged ears, a friend suggested

The name Carmelis combines the names of the Barmors' two daughters, Carmel (above) and Lior

switching the little girl from cow's milk to goat's milk. The change made a big difference in her health, and provided the impetus to change the Barmors from sheep to goat farmers. In the late 1990s, they operated a goat's milk dairy east of Haifa in Israel's Jezreel Valley.

Already thinking that they might like to leave Israel ("It's no place to raise children," says Ofri) the Barmors became inspired by a vacation to the Okanagan Valley in 2002. They loved it so much that they put an offer on a house before returning home. By March of 2003, they'd moved to Kelowna permanently with the intention of starting another goat dairy.

In August of 2003, a raging forest fire destroyed thousands of acres in the Okanagan Valley around Kelowna. The Barmors' home and facilities (still under construction at the time) were directly in the path of the fire; just four days after taking delivery of their first goats, they received an evacuation order. "We had no idea what we were going to do," says Ofri. Friends made phone calls trying to round up help, and Ofer even resorted to calling a local radio station. "Half an hour after the broadcast there were 10 pickups with trailers waiting on the road. We saved all of the goats." The family returned three weeks later and found that their home had survived, but the nascent cheesemaking facilities were completely destroyed. Incredibly, the Barmors persevered. By early November, the goats were back on the property and in February of 2004, the first cheese was finally made at Carmelis Goat Dairy.

The Barmors have not only survived their ordeal, they've prospered as artisan cheesemakers in their adopted country. Only a few years after rebuilding, they're making over a dozen of styles of goat's milk cheeses ranging from delicate soft-ripened cheeses to giant wheels of goat's milk gruyere that please the palates of chefs, consumers, and cheese appreciators. The farm, located in a gorgeous location overlooking Okanagan Lake, welcomes visitors to its popular and well-appointed shop for cheese tastings; visitors can also enjoy the silky goat's milk gelato that Ofri makes several days a week.

The Barmors were sheep farmers in Israel before establishing their popular goat dairy in the Okanagan Valley

12. D DUTCHMEN DAIRY

DeWitt Family

1321 Maeir Rd.

Sicamous, BC V0E 2V0

250-836-4304

dutchmendairy.ca

COW'S MILK, FEDERALLY REGISTERED

VISITORS

Farm open

9 AM–9 PM,

7 days a week

STYLES OF CHEESE

Fresh

Cheese curds

Aged

Cheddar

Gouda

Jack

Mozzarella

(All available in plain and flavored varieties)

Also makes and sells ice cream

D Dutchmen is a familiar sight for travelers on the Trans-Canada Highway in British Columbia

Generations know D Dutchmen as a favorite tourist destination and ice cream shop along the British Columbia portion of the Trans-Canada Highway. Owned by the DeWitt family since 1978, D Dutchmen's primary business is producing bottled milk and dairy products using pooled milk from both the farm's cows and other provincial dairies. A large portion of D Dutchmen's cheese production is sold to the food service industry, but the cheese is made at the farm and is available for sale on-site or in local markets.

13. GORT'S GOUDA

GARY AND KATHY WIKKERINK

1470 50th St. SW

Salmon Arm, BC V1E 3C3

250-832-4274

gortsgoudacheese.bc.ca

COW'S MILK, CERTIFIED ORGANIC,
FEDERALLY REGISTERED

VISITORS

During July and August, open Tuesday,
Wednesday, and Friday at 10 AM, or call
for an appointment. See the Web site or
call for the most up-to-date schedule.

STYLES OF CHEESE

Fresh

Bulgarian-Style Yogurt
Crème Fraîche
Cow and Goat's Milk Feta *(goat feta*
available both plain and flavored)
Quark

Aged

Gouda, mild, medium, aged *(cow and goat's*
milk, plain and flavored)
Maasdammer

A few of Gort's herd of Brown Swiss and Milking
Shorthorn cows

ritish Columbia's first small artisan cheesemaker, Gort's Gouda, was founded by Arie and Anneke Gort in 1983. After leaving Zimbabwe (then Rhodesia) in the late 1970s, the Gort family, native Hollanders, migrated back to their home country for a time before settling permanently on a 44-acre farm in the British Columbia town

Gort's signature Goudas are made with a variety of flavors and are aged to be mild, medium, or sharp

of Salmon Arm in 1981. They started the cheesemaking operation soon after.

In its formative years, Gort's Gouda was a busy family-run operation, with all six Gort children pitching in, helping with animal care and cheesemaking. Initially the Gorts focused solely on Gouda production, but later branched out into other products, including Quark, Bulgarian-style yogurt, and Feta. Gort's signature Gouda won first place in its category in the prestigious Canadian Cheese Grand Prix competition in 2004. About 60 Brown Swiss and Milking Shorthorn cows graze in the farm's gorgeous pastures, ensuring excellent quality milk for Gort's cheeses. All of the farm's products are sold at the on-site shop, a popular attraction just off the Trans-Canada Highway.

In August of 2007, Arie Gort retired from the cheesemaking business, selling the farm and passing the reigns of his successful operation to Gary and Kathy Wikkerink. The Wikkerinks, also of Dutch descent, moved to Salmon Arm from a small farm in Agassiz, in British Columbia's Fraser Valley, and plan to continue Gort's tradition of great cheesemaking. Arie Gort continues to make his mark on cheesemaking throughout the region, offering advice and counsel to cheesemakers in both the United States and Canada who are eager to benefit from his years of experience and success in the industry.

GORT'S GOUDA
CHEESE FARM

14. HAPPY DAYS GOAT DAIRY

DONAT KOLLER

691 Salmon River Rd.

Salmon Arm, BC V1E 4M1

Milk processing facility and cheese shop:

7350A Barrow Rd.

Chilliwack, BC V2R 4J8

604-823-7241

happydaysdairy.com

GOAT'S MILK, FEDERALLY REGISTERED

STYLES OF CHEESE

Fresh

Feta

Fresh Chèvre, marinated in oil and herbs

Mild-aged goat cheese

Okanagan brand Fresh Chèvre

Yogurt

Also sells goat's milk and ice cream

onat Koller is a cheesemaker by training who immigrated to Canada from Switzerland in 1993. "In Switzerland I was an employee, but I wanted to own my own business, so I came to Canada," he says. Koller started in Salmon Arm, British Columbia on a rented farm with a herd of about 70 goats. Although he had originally planned to make cheese, he seized an opportunity in the fluid goat's milk industry and within a few years had developed a substantial business. Today Happy Days Goat Dairy is the dominant presence in the regional goat's milk industry, processing the milk of over 6,000 goats from British Columbia and Alberta at its facility in Chilliwack, British Columbia.

Although milk processing is his primary focus, Koller makes several styles of cheese as well, primarily fresh cheeses like fresh chèvre and feta in addition to yogurt and ice cream. Due to the constraints of managing supply and demand, the majority of the goat's milk he uses goes to the fluid milk and fresh cheeses rather than aged cheeses, which would require storage and attention to affinage. Koller contributes significantly to cheesemaking in British Columbia in another way as well—by offering advice and support to many area artisans. Cheesemaker Paul Sutter of Natural Pastures once worked for Koller, as did Kees Tuijtel of newly formed Triple Island Farm.

15. JERSEYLAND ORGANICS

JEREMY AND KEELY deVRIES

2690 Almond Gardens Rd.

Grand Forks, BC V0H 1H0

250-442-8112

jerseylandorganics.com

COW'S MILK, CERTIFIED ORGANIC, FEDERALLY REGISTERED

STYLES OF CHEESE

Fresh

Yogurt

Aged

Asiago

Cheddar, mild and sharp

Feta

Gouda, plain and flavored

Leicester

Jerseyland owner Jeremy deVries with one of his curious Jersey cows

Jerseyland's origins date back to the 1980s, when Ric and Vickie Llewellyn purchased a farm in Grand Forks, British Columbia, bringing their small herd of Jersey cows along with them. Over time, cowkeeping evolved into a dairy and then into a formal cheesemaking operation in 1995. For 11 years, the Llewellyns made cheese and yogurt from the milk of their growing herd.

One reason the Llewellyns began making cheese was that the local community of Dukhobors (a community of Russian pacifist expatriates who migrated to Western Canada in the late 19th and early 20th century) were looking for someone who could make the kind of cheese they liked. Ric started out making a type of cottage cheese favored by the community, and his cheese business grew from there.

After working for the Llewellyns for several years, Jeremy and wife Keely deVries purchased the business along with its 35 Jersey cows in 2006 and now run Jerseyland Organics full time. Jeremy is a third-generation dairyman of Dutch ancestry originally from the Lower Mainland; both he and Keely are committed to organic and sustainable farming and to continuing the legacy built by the Llewellyns.

Visitors to the Grand Forks area are welcome to stop by and purchase Jerseyland's organic cheeses

16. MOUNTAIN MEADOW SHEEP DAIRY

RR#2 Chase Creek Rd.
Chase, BC V0E 1M0
250-679-3841
sheepcheesecanada.com
SHEEP'S MILK, CERTIFIED ORGANIC

STYLES OF CHEESE

Fresh
Feta
Sheep Droppings
Yogurt
Aged
Aged Sheep's Cheese

Mountain Meadow's dairy sheep graze in the hills near Chase, British Columbia

Hani and Theres Gasser moved to British Columbia from Switzerland and founded Mountain Meadow Sheep Dairy in 1993. For over a decade they made a variety of cheeses, including a memorable sheep's milk brie. In 2006 the Gassers retired, selling their farm and cheese-making operation to a Korean corporation. Since then, the farm has been in transition, making small amounts of cheese and yogurt and selling its products primarily through Vancouver area farmers' markets. According to a representative, the new owners hope to be making cheese on site within the next year or so and have the eventual goal of exporting cheese and dairy products back to Korea.

17. POPLAR GROVE CHEESE COMPANY

GITTA SUTHERLAND

1060 Poplar Grove Rd.

Penticton, BC V2A 8T6

250-492-4575

poplargrovecheese.ca

COW'S MILK, FEDERALLY REGISTERED

Poplar Grove's Harvest Moon is washed regularly with a brine solution, which imparts the characteristic color and flavor

STYLES OF CHEESE

Soft-ripened

Naramata Bench Blue

Okanogan Double Cream Camembert

Washed-rind

Harvest Moon

Blue

Tiger Blue

Gitta Sutherland grew up on a farm in Denmark and immigrated to Canada nearly 20 years ago. She and her former husband, Ian, started Poplar Grove Winery in 1997. Though the Sutherlands pioneered the idea of partnering cheesemaking and winemaking under one umbrella, cheese was not immediately foremost in their minds when they started the winery. It was later, on a trip to Australia, that Gitta met a cheesemaker at Millawa Cheese Company in one of Australia's winemaking regions. Having always been intrigued by the idea of cheesemaking, this proved to be the spark of inspiration

that led to the founding of the winery's sister company, Poplar Grove Cheese Company.

Sutherland played with recipes in her kitchen for a few years, making Camembert-style cheeses in small batches and ripening them in her basement. "I quickly realized that I'd need a more controlled environment to make a consistent product," she laughs. Eventually the Sutherlands added a cheese room onto the winery building and began making cheese in more significant quantities. Several years ago they constructed expanded cheese-making facilities adjacent to the winery tasting room.

Poplar Grove's production is seasonal, increasing in the summer months and dipping a bit in the winter. "We're a very hands-on, small operation," she says. Gitta and several employees take turns making cheese, hooping, washing rinds, and all of the other attendant tasks that go along with making and caring for cheese. While the winery portion of the business was recently sold, Gitta Sutherland remains the owner of Poplar Grove Cheeses and is committed to its continuing success.

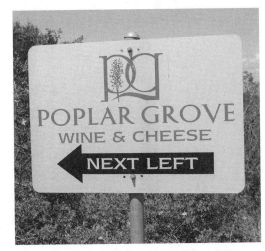

Poplar Grove is a great place to stop for both wine and cheese tasting

18. TRIPLE ISLAND FARM

TUIJTEL FAMILY
1519 Hwy. 6
Lumby, BC V0E 2G1
250-547-6125
COW'S MILK, PROVINCIALLY REGISTERED

STYLES OF CHEESE
Gouda, plain and spiced

Kees Tuijtel holds a wheel of his popular Gouda cheese

The Tuijtel family emigrated from Holland to Canada about nine years ago, settling on their farm near Cherryville, British Columbia, in 2005 and starting cheese production in 2008. Not surprisingly, they've begun making farmstead Gouda cheeses that hearken back to their homeland; British Columbia is home to a significant population of Dutch immigrants so Gouda is always a good choice for area cheesemakers.

Kees (pronounced *case*) is the cheesemaker of the family, making cheese six days a week from the milk of the family's small herd of Holstein cows, currently at 18 and growing. Kees learned the craft by apprenticing in a cheese factory in Holland as well as working with Donat

136

Koller at Happy Days Goat Dairy. Kees says he expects to refine his technique as he goes along and as he learns how the milk and the environment affect his cheeses.

Cheesemaking is still relatively new to the Tuijtels, but they're obviously doing something right since they're selling out of their cheeses at local farmers' markets and at their on-site shop. They hope to eventually develop the farm into a destination for tourists who want to experience a working farm and cheesemaking operation.

Gouda was a natural choice for this Dutch immigrant family

19. THE VILLAGE CHEESE COMPANY

HUBERT AND NORMAN BESNER, CHEESEMAKERS

3475 Smith Dr.

Armstrong, BC V0E 1B0

250-546-8651 or 888-633-8999

villagecheese.com

COW'S MILK, FEDERALLY REGISTERED

STYLES OF CHEESE

Fresh

Cheese curds

Fresh Chèvre

Goat's Milk Feta, plain and flavored

Aged

Cheddar *(multiple varieties)*, **mild, medium, sharp, and extra sharp, aged 1–8 years, both plain and flavored**

Jack

Pale Ale Beer Cheese

Washed-rind

Brick

If you're driving through the Okanagan Valley you're sure to notice signs announcing the presence of The Village Cheese Company as you approach Armstrong, British Columbia. It's an extroverted type of place that draws people in with its promise of "good times, cheese, and ice cream." Once there, you'll find a facility that is determined to deliver an all around cheese experience. Generous windows allow tourists a view onto the cheesemaking floor while a closed loop video describes the process. There's also plenty of opportunity to taste the factory's wide variety of products that include numerous varieties of cheddar, both plain and flavored, some with unique components like maple syrup and smoked salmon. Lunch is served daily and the shop sells cheese as well as ice cream and crafts.

The Village Cheese Company makes several dozen styles of cheese, ensuring that visitors will find one that appeals to them

Dwight Johnson started The Village Cheese Company in 1999, around the same time that community mainstay Armstrong Cheese (in business since the early 1900s) was bought out by industrial giant Saputo and closed down. As a result of Armstrong's demise, Johnson was able to bring experienced cheesemakers into his operation. Though The Village is not shy about marketing to Okanagan Valley tourists, at the same time they are no slouches in the cheesemaking department. Master Cheesemaker Hubert Besner's decades of experience have contributed greatly to the operation's success; more recently son Norman Besner has begun to oversee cheesemaking at the plant.

NEW IN THOMPSON OKANAGAN/KOOTENAYS

20. KOOTENAY ALPINE CHEESE COMPANY

WAYNE AND DENISE HARRIS

3071 16th St.

Lister, BC V0B 1Y0

250-428-9655

kootenayalpinecheese.com

COW'S MILK, FEDERALLY REGISTERED

Dairy farmers Wayne and Denise Harris have been farming near Creston, British Columbia, in the heart of the Kootenays for 16 years. Their farm is situated in a beautiful valley rimmed by mountains reminiscent of a European alpine village. A few years ago, they decided to diversify their dairy operation by trying something new, making cheese. The Harrises started their operation in the fall of 2008, qualifying them as British Columbia's newest artisan cheesemakers, for now. True to the spirit of their surroundings, the Harrises plan to focus on producing Alpine-style raw-milk aged cheeses.

APPENDIXES

GLOSSARY OF CHEESE TERMS

AFFINAGE: The process of caring for cheese as it ages, encompassing a variety of actions, including temperature and humidity controls, as well as manual brushing or washing of rinds.

AFFINEUR: An expert in the art of affinage, this person understands and applies specific techniques that maximize a particular cheese's flavor and character potential.

ARTISAN CHEESE: Cheese made by hand in small batches, with attention to craft and detail not found in industrial level production.

BANDAGE-WRAPPED CHEESE: *See Cloth-bound cheese.*

BLOOMY RIND: *See Soft-ripened cheese.*

BLUE CHEESE: A style of cheese with characteristic visible veins of blue mold; typically has distinct pungent, salty flavors. Blue cheese is made by adding mold spores to milk during the cheesemaking process. Once the cheese is formed, the body is pierced (typically by long needle-like devices) to allow air to penetrate the inside of the wheel, stimulating the growth of the mold.

CHEESE CAVE: Typically temperature and humidity controlled spaces where cheeses are aged. Sometimes these facilities are actual caves (i.e., large openings in the earth, as in Roquefort, France). The term is used more often to affectionately refer to an aging room or refrigerated storage area.

CHÈVRE: The French word for "goat"; fresh goat's milk cheeses are typically called *chèvre* in North America, although the term is technically correct when used for any type of goat cheese. Fresh chèvre has a characteristic tart, dairy flavor profile.

CLOTH-BOUND CHEESE: Some cheeses, particularly Cheddars aged for several years, are wrapped in cheesecloth before storing, which protects the rind. The cloth-bound cheese is typically wiped or coated with butter or lard for further protection and flavor development. Also called bandage-wrapped cheese. *See Rind.*

CURD: When a coagulating agent, such as bacterial culture and/or rennet, is added to milk, the milk solids separate from the liquid whey. These remaining milk solids, termed *curds,* will vary in texture from light and fluffy to solid and slippery or squeaky, depending on a variety of factors, including the type of cheese being made. Cheese curds are often sold as a distinct product, but more typically represent a stage in the cheesemaking process, and may be treated in a variety of ways (including pressing and heating) to achieve the desired end result.

FARMSTEAD CHEESE: Cheese made from milk that comes from the farm where the cheese is made. Analogous to the wine term *estate-bottled.*

FEDERAL REGISTRATION: A Canadian regulatory category administered at the national level by the Canadian Food Inspection Agency (CFIA). Cheesemakers that are federally registered are able to sell their products across Canada as well as to export across international boundaries. *See Provincial registration.*

FRESH CHEESE: Unripened cheese that is ready to eat immediately or nearly immediately after it is made. Typically cheeses made in this style are simply flavored, moist cheeses with tart dairy flavors, such as paneer, cottage cheese, or fresh mozzarella. *See Chèvre and Fromage blanc.*

FROMAGE BLANC: Literally translated from its French name, *fromage blanc* is simply "white cheese." Fromage blanc is a fresh, unripened cheese with a soft, spreadable texture and mild flavor. Also referred to as *fromage frais* or "fresh cheese".

MOLD-RIPENED CHEESE: A style of cheese characterized by the presence of molds that act as agents in the ripening (or aging) of the cheese. *See Surface-ripened cheese.*

NATURAL RIND: *See Rind.*

PASTE: Cheese professionals often refer to the flesh or body of a cheese as its paste (distinguished from the outside, or rind).

PASTEURIZATION: In the 19th century, Louis Pasteur developed the process that now bears his name as a means to destroy harmful pathogens in perishable liquids, including milk.

Today state, provincial, and federal authorities strictly regulate pasteurization. The process of dairy pasteurization consists of heating milk to a temperature sufficient to kill bacteria while at the same time preserving the integrity of the milk proteins. Some of the most commonly employed types of pasteurization include:

Vat Pasteurization (LTLT or low temperature long time)

The most common type of pasteurization used by small artisan cheesemakers. Milk is held in a large vat at a minimum of 145 degrees Fahrenheit for 30 minutes.

HTST (High Temperature Short Time)

Also known as plate pasteurization or continuous pasteurization. Commonly used in larger cheesemaking operations; in this process milk is forced through a series of metal plates and heated to a minimum of 161 degrees Fahrenheit for at least 15 seconds. This process is efficient for larger operations because large quantities of milk can be processed quickly and continuously.

Ultra Pasteurization (UHT)

A process developed to increase the shelf life of milk, ultra-pasteurized milk is held at 280 degrees Fahrenheit for at least two seconds. Because this process denatures milk proteins, it is not typically used in the cheesemaking process.

Thermalization (Heat Shock)

In this process, milk is heated to a lower temperature than traditional pasteurization, but for a longer period of time. Practitioners believe that by minimizing heat they will preserve beneficial bacteria and enzymes as well as milk protein structure while at the same time any destroying harmful pathogens. Thermalization does not fall under the definition of pasteurization employed by regulatory authorities in the United States or Canada; cheeses made with this milk must be aged a minimum of 60 days to be sold. *See Raw-milk cheese.*

PROVINCIAL REGISTRATION: A Canadian regulatory category administered at the provincial level. Provincial registration enables cheesemakers to make and sell cheese only within the province in which they operate. Smaller farms and dairies are often licensed under this category. *See Federal registration.*

RAW-MILK CHEESE: Cheese made from milk that has not been pasteurized. In the United States and most of Canada, laws require raw-milk cheeses to be aged for at least 60 days at a minimum of 35 degrees Fahrenheit in order to be sold commercially. *See Pasteurization.*

RENNET: Often thought of as a specific substance, the term *rennet* actually refers to any of a collection of enzymes, primarily chymosin, used to coagulate milk as part of the cheesemaking process. There are several different sources of rennet used in modern cheesemaking:

Animal rennet

Traditional rennet is an animal product consisting of coagulating enzymes recovered from the stomachs of young calves, lambs, and goat kids. Chymosin is the primary enzyme component in animal rennet.

GMO Fermentation rennet

Because of the limited availability of animal rennet, scientists have developed so-called GMO rennet, which is produced by bacteria whose DNA has been altered to include genetic material from animals, causing the bacteria to produce pure chymosin.

Microbial rennet

Coagulating enzymes recovered from a specific species of fungus; resembles chymosin, but are not exactly the same chemically.

Vegetable rennet

Some plants from the thistle family contain enzymes that have traditionally been used as coagulants in the cheesemaking process. Spain and Portugal in particular make outstanding thistle-rennet cheeses such as Sera de Estrella.

RIND: The outer surface of a cheese. A natural-rind cheese is one that has aged with its rind exposed to air during the aging process; as a result, various microorganisms may also grow on the surface of the cheese and act to age and flavor the cheese, creating a rough surface, or rind, that acts as protection for the cheese inside. In contrast, non-natural-rind cheeses may be coated with wax or another similar substance or vacuum packed in plastic to prevent damage while aging. *See Cloth-bound cheese.*

RIPENING: Technically speaking, ripening is a stage in the cheesemaking process, occurring after an acidifying agent (typically bacteria) is added to the milk. After this stage, rennet is added to coagulate the milk proteins.

The term *ripening* is more commonly used to refer to the cheese aging process. Once a cheese is physically made, there is generally a period of time when it must age, or ripen, to reach its maximum potential. The time varies widely depending on the style. Soft-ripened cheeses may reach their peak after just two to three weeks; some cheddars, on the other hand, may not be fully ripe until after two years or more.

The process of caring for a cheese during the ripening/aging process is called *affinage*.

SOFT-RIPENED CHEESE: Typically a young cheese (French-made Brie and Camembert are the most recognizable cheeses in this style). During the aging process, these cheeses develop a whitish rind, which is sometimes referred to as a bloomy rind. These cheeses ripen from the outside in and often have a creamy, soft paste. *See also Surface-ripened cheese.*

STINKY CHEESE: *See Washed-rind cheese.*

SURFACE-RIPENED CHEESE: Any style of cheese that ripens from the outside in is a surface-ripened cheese, including soft-ripened and washed-rind cheeses. Ripening occurs due in large part to the action of various fungal microorganisms such as *Penicillum camemberti* or *Geotrichum candidum*. *See also Soft-ripened cheese.*

TERROIR: French word for "terrain." In the cheese world, the term is used to describe the particular nuances of place, such as regional environment, pasture conditions, soil composition, which are said to be expressed in a farm's milk and in the resulting cheese made from that milk.

TOMME: A traditional French term used to denote cheeses from the Alpine regions made with skim milk. This term is most often used in North America to refer to a broad category of aged, natural-rind cheeses.

TRUCKLE: A term used to refer to cheese made in a barrel or cylindrical shape.

WASHED-RIND CHEESE: A style of cheese so named because its rind is washed, typically with a brine solution or alcohol, during the aging process. The treatment encourages the growth of various microorganisms that contribute to the flavor and complexity of the finished product. Perhaps the most familiar style of washed-rind cheeses are those coated with *B. linens* bacteria, which lends an orange color and so-called stinky aroma, often compared to smelly socks.

WHEY: A by-product of the cheesemaking process, whey refers to the yellowish liquid that separates from the milk proteins (curds) when the milk coagulates. Whey is sometimes used by cheesemakers to feed their dairy animals, spread on fields as fertilizer, or may be consumed by humans as a nutritional supplement. Whey contains some nutritional elements, including proteins and minerals, that are not recovered during the cheesemaking process. Cheesemakers take advantage of this by making cheese from whey—traditional Italian ricotta is one example of a whey cheese.

CHEESE BASICS

*M*y formative experiences with cheese centered around two orange products: the bright orange freeze-dried powder integral to my favorite childhood dish, macaroni and cheese, and the rubbery stuff that still comes in individually wrapped slices. Perhaps you were once as attached to those so-called cheeses as I was. Now that all of us are grown up and are interested in making better cheese choices, it doesn't take long to see that the cheese world is much more complicated than we were prepared for. A well-stocked cheese counter, with its eye-catching range of styles and choices from all over the world, can be overwhelming and more than a little bit daunting.

The truth is this, like many good things, the world of cheese is an easy one to explore, if approached with an open mind and a sense of adventure. By taking the time to learn a few basic principles you can take these tools with you on your cheese explorations. Soon enough you'll be converting your friends to the joys of artisan cheese.

STYLE PRIMER

Experts typically divide cheeses into several distinct categories: fresh, soft-ripened, washed-rind, blue, semi-soft, semi-hard, and hard. While to some extent these categories overlap and can be loosely defined, they are a convenient way to start wrapping your mind around the types of cheese that are out there.

FRESH

Fresh cheeses are as close to fresh milk you can get and still call it cheese. Typically just days or weeks old, they are simply made and reflect the fresh dairy flavors of the milk. Styles may range from spreadable cheeses like fresh chèvre (made with goat's milk) or fromage blanc, cottage cheese, fresh mozzarella, or queso fresco.

Because of its simplicity, fresh cheese is a tempting blank canvas for cheesemakers, who often add sweet or savory flavors. You'll often find fresh chèvre, for example, sold plain as well as flavored with herbs, spices, or sweet flavorings.

NORTHWEST CHEESES IN THIS STYLE:

Cow's Milk

Oregon Gourmet Cheese Fromage Blanc (OR), Willamette Valley Cheese Company Queso Fresco (OR), Queseria Bendita Requeson (WA), Appel Farms Quark (WA), The Farm House Natural Cheeses Fromage Frais (BC)

Goat's Milk

Most goat cheese makers make a fresh chèvre or fromage blanc as part of their repertoire of offerings; look for fresh cheeses from Rivers Edge Chèvre (OR), Juniper Grove Farm (OR), Port Madison Farm (WA), Gothberg Farms (WA), Rollingstone Chèvre (ID), Salt Spring Island Cheese Co (BC), and Carmelis Goat Cheese (BC).

Sheep's Milk

Black Sheep Creamery Ricotta (WA), Mountain Meadow Sheep Droppings (BC)

SOFT-RIPENED

Soft-ripened cheeses possess a characteristic whitish, edible rind formed by the action of various types of molds such as *Penicillum candidum*. Soft-ripened cheeses ripen from the outside in due to the activity of these microorganisms on the surface of the cheese. While French-made Brie or Camembert are two of this style that may be most familiar, Northwest producers make dozens of varieties of soft-ripened cheeses. These cheeses are often referred to as bloomy-rind cheeses.

NORTHWEST CHEESES IN THIS STYLE:

Cow's Milk

Mt. Townsend Creamery Cirrus (WA); Oregon Gourmet Camembert (OR), Willamette Valley Cheese Company French Brie (OR); The Farm House Natural Cheeses Brie (BC), Natural Pastures Comox Brie (BC)

Goat's Milk

Rivers Edge Mary's Peak (OR); Monteillet Fromagerie Larzac (WA); Carmelis Goat Cheese makes a variety of soft-ripened cheeses including Chabichu and Misty (BC); Hilary's St. Michel (BC)

Sheep's Milk

Ancient Heritage Valentine (OR); Monteillet Fromagerie Mejean (WA)

WASHED-RIND

Washed-rind cheeses are, as the name suggests, literally washed during the aging process. Cheesemakers may wash cheeses by hand or mechanically with a variety of substances, including saltwater brine, oils, wine or other spirits. These cheeses are often called "stinky" cheeses because the washing of rinds encourages the growth of a particular type of bacteria called *Brevibacterium linens,* which produces a distinctive odor and a typically strong, salty flavor. Not all washed-rind cheeses will be strong tasting or smelly, however.

NORTHWEST CHEESES IN THIS STYLE:

Cow's Milk

Estrella Family Creamery Valentina (WA), The Farm House Natural Cheeses Alpine Gold (BC), Poplar Grove Harvest Moon (BC)

Goat's Milk

Juniper Grove Farm Tumalo Tomme (OR), Estrella Family Creamery Caldwell Crick Chèvrette (Cow / Goat's Milk blend) (WA)

Sheep's Milk
>   Ancient Heritage Opal Creek (sheep/cow's milk blend) (OR)

SEMI-SOFT

Semi-soft cheeses are, as their name implies, cheeses that fall on the soft, pliable side of the texture spectrum. They're typically younger cheeses that have retained more moisture than their aged cousins and as a result their texture is smooth and creamy. These cheeses are often mild in flavor, easy to eat and often used in cooking.

NORTHWEST CHEESES IN THIS STYLE:

Cow's Milk
>   Willamette Valley Cheese Company Havarti (OR), Samish Bay Cheese Company Port Edison (WA), Ballard Family Dairy Idaho Jersey Gem (ID), Gort's Mild Gouda (BC)

Goat's Milk
>   Fraga Farm Goatzarella (OR)

Sheep's Milk
>   Sally Jackson Leaf Wrapped Sheep Cheese (WA)

SEMI-HARD

Semi-hard cheeses are aged several months or more. The aging process causes the cheeses to lose moisture and as a result, these cheeses tend to be—you guessed it—firmer, more compact, and denser in texture. Texture is not by itself an indicator of flavor, however, and the taste of these cheeses can range from mild to pungent.

NORTHWEST CHEESES IN THIS STYLE:

Cow's Milk
>   Oregon Gourmet Sublimity (OR), Washington State University Cougar Gold (WA),

Mt. Townsend Creamery Trailhead (WA), Ballard Family Dairy White Cheddar (ID), Gort's Maasdammer (BC)

Goat's Milk

Fraga Farm Rio Santiam (OR), Tumalo Farms Classico (OR), Quillisascut Curado (WA), Steamboat Island Goat Farm Cheddar (WA), Hilary's Belle Ann (BC)

Sheep's Milk

Willamette Valley Cheese Company Perrydale (cow/sheep's milk blend) (OR), Ancient Heritage Hannah Bridge Heritage (OR), Black Sheep Creamery Mopsy's Best (WA), Salt Spring Island Cheese Company Montaña (BC).

HARD

As a cheese ages, it loses moisture and typically becomes progressively more firm. Familiar cheeses like the Italian Parmigiano-Reggiano fall into this category; these cheeses are typically aged a year or even more. Aged cheeses typically have stronger, more concentrated flavors than their younger cousins. Their texture is crumbly and these cheeses are often good grating cheeses.

NORTHWEST CHEESES IN THIS STYLE:

Cow's Milk

Willamette Valley Cheese Company Aged Gouda (OR), Beecher's Flagship Reserve (WA)

Goat's Milk

Juniper Grove Farm Redmondo (OR), Pine Stump Farms Parmesan (WA), Rollingstone Chèvre Idaho Goatster (ID), Carmelis Goat Cheese Carmel (BC)

BLUE

Blue cheeses are easy to spot because of the streaks of blue mold running through the body of the cheese. To make these cheeses cheesemakers add mold spores to the milk during the cheesemaking process. Once the cheeses are pressed and shaped, they are pierced with needle-like devices to introduce air into the cheese, a process that encourages interior mold growth. Blue cheeses are often, though not always, strongly flavored and possess a characteristic peppery bite.

NORTHWEST CHEESES IN THIS STYLE:

Cow's Milk

Rogue Creamery makes a range of blue cheeses, including Oregon Blue, Oregonzola, Crater Lake Blue and Rogue River Blue (OR), Estrella Family Creamery Wynoochee River Blue (WA); Moonstruck Beddis Blue and Blossom's Blue (BC)

Goat's Milk

Rogue Creamery Echo Mountain Blue (OR) (goat and cow's milk blend), Carmelis Goatgonzola (BC), Goat's Pride Blue Capri (BC)

GUIDELINES FOR BUYING, STORING, AND EATING CHEESE

All cheeses, from the simplest fresh chèvre to aged cheddars have something in common: each is the end product of a complex set of interactions between milk, microorganisms, enzymes, and the environment. These interactions never cease—that's why it's often said that cheese is a living thing. Even when you are observing a hunk of cheese sitting in a cheese case at your local cheese shop, it's still a dynamic, living, and breathing thing that requires nurturing and care.

BUYING CHEESE

If you live in a town that has a cheesemonger or cheese shop that will cut cheese from a wheel to order, this is the ideal. Make sure your cheesemonger wraps the freshly cut cheese in breathable paper, then take your parcel home and consume it within a few days, at its maximum freshness and flavor. Buy cheese in small amounts rather than large quantities. Make friends with your cheesemonger, because he or she knows cheese and will sell you cheeses when they're at their peak.

CARING FOR AND STORING CHEESE

Whether out of necessity or convenience, many of us purchase cheese wrapped in plastic, or wrap cheese in plastic once we've got it home. Plastic is simple, convenient, and enables retailers to give customers a visual of what a cut cheese looks like. The problem with plastic is that it does not allow cheese to breathe and locks in moisture that can accelerate deterioration of the cheese. Some also feel that plastic transmits faint petroleum flavors to the cheese it wraps.

To keep your cheese in top condition, use plastic sparingly with cheese and avoid it completely, if you can. The ideal way to wrap and store most cheeses is to use breathable cheese paper; failing that, wrap a layer of wax or parchment paper over the cheese and cover that layer with plastic. Store oozier soft-ripened and washed-rind cheeses in a plastic container with a lid.

Many people wonder what to do when mold appears on their stored cheese. Most of the time this mold is a harmless by product of the complex interactions between cheese and its environment (remember, cheese is a living thing); simply cut the mold off and enjoy.

SERVING CHEESE

Cheese should *always* be served and enjoyed at room temperature. Your mouth perceives temperature before taste; as a result your experience of a cheese's flavor right out of the refrigerator will be blunted by cold; you'll experience all of the nuances and complexities of a cheeses' flavor if you leave it out for an hour or so before cutting and plating.

Constructing a cheese plate can be as simple as serving a few slices of your favorite local cheese with an accompaniment of chutney or toasted nuts, or serving a selection of five local goat's milk cheeses and taking notes on the variances in flavor, texture and complexity of each.

Generally a cheese plate works best if you limit its scope to avoid risk of palate overload. Choose three to five cheeses and include a range of styles, perhaps a soft-ripened style, a semi-firm style, and a denser, more aged cheese, or a blue. Serve fresh bread, crackers, and fruit on the side as palate cleansers. Accompaniments like dried fruits (figs and apricots) and chutneys are also tasty.

PAIRING CHEESE WITH WINE, BEER, AND OTHER SPIRITS

For the uninitiated, pairing cheese and spirits can seem complicated; novices often fear that they won't do it right. In fact, pairing beverages and cheeses is really as simple as being present to the flavors your mouth is experiencing.

Start out with this principle: a good pairing is one where the flavors of both the beverage and the cheese are enhanced by the combination. In the best pairings, you may find that the pairing produces a remarkable transformation on your palate, and a third flavor revelation emerges. Bad pairings are easy to discern and will almost certainly cause your mouth to screw up involuntarily in odd contortions as a result of the bitter, awkward flavors generated in your mouth. In fact, bad pairings are one easy way to start educating yourself about the ins and outs of pairing cheese and wine. Try a few pairings of wine and cheese, even random ones, and start paying attention to how the combinations fit into these broad categories.

Wine is the classic beverage for pairing with cheese, but that's only the beginning. Some find that beer pairs well, if not better, than wine. Other beverages such as sake, cider, and lambic ales can also be nicely paired with cheese. More recently, people are beginning to experiment with pairing coffee and cheese, as well as whiskey and cheese.

Following are a few basic pairing principles to start you on your pairing adventures:

Trust Your Own Palate

Pairings are *very* subjective, and despite what anyone tells you, there are no right or wrong answers—really. The very same pairing may be transcendent to some and unpalatable to others. For example, many people find red wines difficult to pair with cheese because of the predominance of tannin; others enjoy such pairings with full-flavored cheeses, such as washed-rinds or strong blues.

Pair Like with Like

Pay attention to the relative intensity of the flavors you are pairing. Generally speaking, very strong flavored cheeses paired with light, dry libations won't work because the cheese will overpower the wine. By the same token, a big red wine, like Barolo, will drown out a subtly flavored soft-ripened goat cheese. Pairing this way does neither product a favor. That being said, see the next rule.

Be Open to the Unexpected

Whatever rules you might have learned may prove false with any given pairing at any given time. Cheese flavors vary throughout the year due to the diet of the animals and seasonal variations in butterfat content of milk; wines and beers also vary by vintage and by batch. In addition, counterintuitive pairings often work very well. For example, ports typically pair well with strongly flavored blue cheeses. You just never know.

ADDITIONAL RESOURCES

The All American Cheese and Wine Book by Laura Werlin, Stewart, Tabori, and Chang, 2003.

Cheese and Wine: Perfect Pairings for Entertaining and Everyday by Janet Fletcher, Chronicle Books, 2007.

The Cheese Plate by Max McCalman and David Gibbons, Clarkson Potter, 2002.

The Cheese Course by Janet Fletcher, Chronicle Books, 2000.

Laura Werlin's Cheese Essentials: An Insider's Guide to Buying and Serving Cheese by Laura Werlin, Stewart, Tabori, and Chang, 2007.

WHERE TO BUY LOCALLY MADE ARTISAN CHEESE

SPECIALTY CHEESE SHOPS AND RETAILERS

Here in the Pacific Northwest, we are blessed with a multitude of specialty grocers that carry artisan-made products, including artisan cheese. Cheese shops, delis, local grocers, and co-ops have responded to consumers' demand for local, handmade products and as a result it is fairly easy to find and buy local artisan cheese even in small communities.

FARMERS' MARKETS

One great way to discover a variety of local cheeses is to visit local farmers' markets. Cheese-makers often attend farmers' markets and they're happy to chat with cheese enthusiasts and answer your questions about their cheeses and cheesemaking. Best of all, at farmers' markets you are buying cheese directly from the producers themselves. Before you go, check an individual market's Web site or call ahead for vendor information and seasonal availability.

DIRECTLY FROM THE CHEESEMAKER

Some artisan cheesemakers welcome visitors and sell cheese at on-farm stores. Where applicable, I've noted shop or farm hours in each profile. If you go, be sure to visit the farm's Web site, or call ahead for current availability and hours. Be a courteous consumer—don't visit a farm without verifying that you are welcome.

Other cheesemakers sell cheese directly from their Web sites regularly or seasonally. Some without Web-enabled ordering may be willing to ship cheese directly to you if you call and make arrangements to pay. Note that regulations prohibit most cheesemakers from shipping cheese across international boundaries (including between Canada and the United States), or between provinces in Canada, if the cheesemaker is Provincially registered.

OREGON

PORTLAND AREA

ELEPHANT'S DELI
www.elephantsdeli.com
503-224-3955
Several locations in the Portland Area

FOOD FRONT
foodfront.coop
2375 NW Thurman St.
Portland, Oregon 97210
503-222-5658

FOSTER & DOBBS
fosteranddobbs.com
2518 NE 15th Ave.
Portland, OR 97212
503-284-1157

PASTAWORKS
www.pastaworks.com
866-206-1735
Several locations in the Portland area.

PEOPLE'S CO-OP
peoples.coop
3029 SE 21st Ave.
Portland, OR 97202
503-674-2642

STEVE'S CHEESE
stevescheese.biz
2321 NW Thurman St.
Portland, OR 97210
503-222-6014

Additional retailers include New Seasons, Whole Foods, Zupan's, and Market of Choice; all have multiple locations in the Portland area.

WILLAMETTE VALLEY

CAPELLA MARKET
capellamarket.com
2489 Willamette St.
Eugene, OR 97405
541-345-1014

FIRST ALTERNATIVE CO-OP
firstalt.coop
541-753-3115
Two stores in the Corvallis area.

THE HORSE RADISH CHEESE AND WINE BAR
thehorseradish.com
211 W Main St.
Carlton, OR 97111
503-852-6656

THE KIVA
kivagrocery.com
125 W 11th Ave.
Eugene, OR 97401
541-342-8666

MARCHE PROVISIONS
marcheprovisions.com
296 E 5th Ave.
Eugene, OR 97401
541-342-3612
Inside the 5th St. Market.

MARKET OF CHOICE
marketofchoice.com
541-345-3349
Several locations in the Eugene area.

NEW FRONTIER MARKET
1101 W 8th Ave.
Eugene, OR 97402
541-345-7401

SUNDANCE NATURAL FOODS
sundancenaturalfoods.com
748 E 24th Ave.
Eugene, OR 97405
541-343-9142

CENTRAL OREGON

ALLYSON'S KITCHEN
allysonskitchen.com
375 SW Powerhouse Dr.
Bend, OR 97702
541-749-9974

NEWPORT AVENUE MARKET
newportavemarket.com
1121 NW Newport Ave.
Bend, Oregon 97701
541-382-3940

OREGON COAST

CHEESE AND CRACKERS
cheeseandcrackersonline.com
373 N Hwy. 101, Suite B
Yachats, OR 97498
541-547-3123

NYE BEACH GALLERY
715 NW 3rd St.
Newport, OR 97365
541-265-3292

OCEANA NATURAL FOODS
oceanafoods.org
159 SE 2nd St.
Newport, OR 97365
541-265-8285

SOUTHERN OREGON

ALLYSON'S KITCHEN
allysonskitchen.com
115 E Main St.
Ashland, OR 97520
541-482-2884

ASHLAND FOOD CO-OP
ashlandfood.coop
237 N 1st St.
Ashland, OR 97520
541-482-2237

MARKET OF CHOICE
marketofchoice.com
1475 Siskiyou Blvd.
Ashland, OR 97520
541-488-2773

ROGUE CREAMERY STORE
roguecreamery.com
311 N Front St.
Central Point, OR 97502
866-665-1155

OREGON'S FARMERS' MARKETS

For a complete list of Oregon farmers' markets across the state, including individual Web sites, locations, and contact information, see the Oregon Farmers' Markets Association Web site at www.oregonfarmersmarkets.org.

WASHINGTON

SEATTLE/PUGET SOUND/SAN JUAN ISLANDS

BEECHER'S HANDMADE CHEESE
beechershandmadecheese.com
1600 Pike Place
Seattle, WA 98101
206-956-1964

BAYLEAF FINE WINES AND IMPORTED FOODS
bayleaf.us
360-678-6603
Two locations on Whidbey Island.

BELLA COSA FOODS
bellacosafoods.com
1711 N 45th St.
Seattle, WA 98103
206-545-7375

THE CHEESE CELLAR
thecheesecellar.com
100 4th Ave. N Suite 150
Seattle, WA 98109
206-404-2743

DELAURENTI SPECIALTY FOOD & WINE
delaurenti.com
1435 1st Ave.
Seattle, WA 98101
800-873-6685

KING'S MARKET
kings-market.com
1620 Spring St.
Friday Harbor, WA 98250
360-378-4505

MADISON MARKET
madisonmarket.com
1600 E Madison St.
Seattle, WA 98122
206-329-1545

OLYMPIA FOOD CO-OP

olympiafood.coop
3111 Pacific Ave. SE
Olympia, WA 98501
360-956-3870

Also at:
921 Rogers St. NW
Olympia, WA 98502
360-754-7666

Additional retailers include Central Market, PCC Natural Markets, Pasta & Company, Metropolitan Market, Town & Country Markets, Thriftway Markets, and Whole Foods; all have multiple area locations.

NORTHWEST WASHINGTON

COMMUNITY FOOD CO-OP

communityfood.coop
1220 N Forest St.
Bellingham, WA 98225
360-734-8158

EVERYBODY'S STORE

everybodys.com
5465 Potter Rd.
Deming, WA 98244
866-832-4695

QUEL FROMAGE

quelfromage.com
1200 Old Fairhaven Pkwy., Suite 101
Bellingham, WA 98225
360-671-0203

THE RESIDENT CHEESEMONGER

residentcheesemonger.com
405 Main St.
Edmonds, WA 98020
425-640-8949

SKAGIT VALLEY CO-OP

skagitfoodcoop.com
202 S 1st St.
Mt. Vernon, WA 98273
360-336-9777

SLOUGH FOOD

sloughfood.com
5766 Cain's Ct., Suite B
Edison, WA 98232
360-766-4458

Additional retailers include Haagen's and Thriftway Stores; both have multiple locations.

EASTERN WASHINGTON

FRESH ABUNDANCE

freshabundance.com
509-533-2724
Two locations in Spokane area.

HUCKLEBERRY'S NATURAL MARKET

huckleberrysnaturalmarket.com
926 S Monroe St.
Spokane, WA 99204
509-624-1349

SALUMIERE CESARIO

salumierecesario.com
20 N 2nd Ave.
Walla Walla, WA 99362
509-529-5620

SAUNDERS CHEESE MARKET

saunderscheesemarket.com
210 S Washington St.
Spokane, WA 99201
509-455-9400

Additional retailers include Top Food & Drug, Yoke's Fresh Markets, and Thriftway Stores; all have multiple locations.

WASHINGTON FARMERS' MARKETS

For a complete List of Farmers' Markets in Washington, including individual Web sites and contact information, see the Washington State Farmers' Markets Association Web site at wafarmersmarkets.com.

IDAHO

BLUE RIBBON ARTISANS CREAMERY

blueribbonartisans.com
1441 N Eagle Rd.
Meridian, ID 83642
208-855-5800

BOISE CO-OP

boisecoop.com
888 W Fort St.
Boise, ID 83702
208- 472-4500

MOSCOW FOOD CO-OP

moscowfood.coop
121 E 5th St.
Moscow, ID 83843
208-882-8537

RUDY'S: A COOK'S PARADISE

cooksparadise.com
147 Main Ave. W
Twin Falls, ID 83301
208-733-5477

Additional retailers include Atkinson's, Ridley's Foods, and Yoke's Fresh Markets; all have multiple locations in Idaho.

IDAHO FARMERS' MARKETS

For a complete list of Idaho Farmers' Markets, including locations and contact information, see the Idaho Department of Agriculture's listing available at: www.agri.state.id.us/Categories/Marketing/FM marketing.php.

BRITISH COLUMBIA
VANCOUVER / FRASER VALLEY

BENTON BROTHERS FINE CHEESE
bentonscheese.com
2104 W 41st Ave.
Vancouver, BC V6M 1Z1
604-261-5813

DUSSA'S HAM AND CHEESE
1689 Johnson St.
Vancouver, BC V6H 3R9
604-688-8881
In the Granville Island Public Market.

EAST END FOOD CO-OP
east-end-food.coop
1034 Commercial Dr.
Vancouver, BC V5L 3W9
604-254-5044

LA GROTTA DEL FORMAGGIO
1791 Commercial Dr.
Vancouver, BC V5N 4A4
604-255-3911

LES AMIS DU FROMAGE
buycheese.com
1752 W 2nd Ave.
Vancouver, BC V6J 1H6
604-732-4218
Also at:
#518 Park Royal S
Vancouver, BC V7T 2W4
604-925-4218

MAINLY ORGANICS
4348 Main St.
Vancouver, BC V5V 3P9
604-872-3446

MEINHARDT FINE FOODS
meinhardt.com
3002 Granville St.
Vancouver, BC V6H 3J8
604-732-4405

MOUNT PLEASANT CHEESE
mountpleasantcheese.com
3432 Cambie St.
Vancouver, BC V5Z 2W8
604-875-6363

OYAMA SAUSAGE COMPANY
oyamasausage.ca
1689 Johnson St.
Vancouver, BC V6H 3R9
604-327-7407
Inside the Granville Island Public Market.

PANE E FORMAGGIO
pane-e-formaggio.com
4532 W 10th St.
Vancouver, BC V6R 2J1
604-224-1643

URBAN FARE
urbanfare.com
605-975-7550
Several locations in Vancouver area.

Additional retailers include Choices Markets, Save On Food, Whole Foods, and Capers; all have multiple locations in the Vancouver area.

VANCOUVER ISLAND/ GULF ISLANDS

EDIBLE ISLAND WHOLE FOODS MARKET
edibleisland.ca
477 6th St.
Courtenay, BC V9N 6V4
250-334-3116

HILARY'S CHEESE AND DELI
1737 Cowichan Bay Rd.
Cowichan Bay, BC V0R 1N2
250-748-5992

MARKET ON YATES/MILLSTREAM
marketonyates.com
903 Yates St.
Victoria, BC V8V 3M4
250-381-6000
Also at:
125-2401C Millstream Rd.
Victoria, BC V9B 3R5
250-391-1110

OTTAVIO ITALIAN BAKERY AND DELICATESSEN
ottaviovictoria.com
2272 Oak Bay Ave.
Victoria, BC V8R 1G7
250-592-4080

SALT SPRING NATUREWORKS
116 Lower Ganges Rd.
Salt Spring Island, BC V8K 2S8
250-537-2325

Additional retailers with multiple locations on the islands include Thrifty Foods, Quality Foods, Lifestyle Markets, and Save On Foods.

THOMPSON OKANAGAN/KOOTENAYS

THE BENCH ARTISAN FOOD MARKET
thebenchmarket.com
368 Vancouver Ave.
Penticton, BC V2A 1A5
250-492-2222

NATURE'S FARE
naturesfare.com
250-542-5910
Several locations in Okanagan Valley.

OKANAGAN GROCERY
okanagangrocery.com
2355 Gordon Dr.
Kelowna, BC V1W 3X7
250-862-2811

QUALITY GREENS FARM MARKET
qualitygreens.com
250-979-1380
Several locations in Okanagan Valley.

Additional retailers include Choices and Save On Foods; both have multiple locations in the Okanagan region.

BRITISH COLUMBIA FARMERS' MARKETS

For a complete list of farmers' markets in British Columbia, including individual Web sites and contact information, see the BC Association of Farmers' Markets Web site at bcfarmersmarket.org.

RECIPES

SMALL PLATES

FAUX FONDUE
COURTESY SCOTT DOLICH, PARK KITCHEN, PORTLAND

⅓ cup butter
⅓ cup hazelnut flour
1 tsp all-purpose flour
2 tbsp white wine (crisp and dry)
2 cups Willamette Valley Cheese Company Brindisi Fontina, grated
Salt and pepper to taste

Melt the butter in a stainless steel saucepan. Whisk in both flours and whisk continuously over medium heat for 5 minutes, or until the mixture looks like wet sand. Add the white wine and cook for another 5 minutes on medium heat. Whisk in the cheese and turn heat to low. Season with salt and pepper. Adjust the consistency with a bit of white wine or water. Keep sauce covered in a warm place until serving.

TO SERVE: Blanch and shock a bunch of rapini or broccoli, suitably trimmed. Heat a bit of butter in a pan and sauté the cooked rapini or broccoli until it is lightly browned. Place the cooked vegetables on a plate and pour a bit of the cheese sauce over them. You can garnish this dish with toasted hazelnuts or, for meat lovers, a bit of sliced ham.

SMOKED CHÈVRE IN TOMATO SAUCE
COURTESY LAURA BYRNE RUSSELL

- 1 tbsp olive oil
- ½ cup diced onion
- 1 clove garlic, thinly sliced
- 1 16-oz can diced tomatoes with puree
- ¼ tsp salt
- ¼ tsp black pepper
- One crottin River's Edge Up In Smoke chèvre (4 ounces), or other fresh chèvre*
- 2 tsp fresh thyme
- Toasted baguette slices, for serving

In a small saucepan, heat the oil over moderate heat. Add the onion and cook, stirring occasionally, until the onion softens, about 10 minutes. Stir in the garlic and cook for an additional minute. Add the tomatoes, salt, and pepper and simmer until the sauce thickens, about 15 minutes. Set aside to cool. (The sauce can be made 2 days ahead and kept covered in the refrigerator.)

Heat the oven to 350°F. Divide the cooled tomato sauce between two small oval ramekins.** Slice the cheese in half horizontally. In each of the baking dishes, nest one slice of cheese in the tomato sauce. (The sauce should just reach the top of the cheese.) Bake until the cheese is warm and the sauce is bubbling, 20–25 minutes. Sprinkle the chopped thyme over the cheese and sauce. Serve on toasted baguette slices.

Serves 6 as an appetizer.

* If you can't find smoked chèvre, use 4 ounces of plain chèvre, cut into 2 2-ounce pieces. In addition, add ¼ teaspoon smoked paprika (pimenton de la vera) to the sauce along with the tomatoes for a smoky flavor.

** You can use one larger baking dish. The sauce should come up just to the top of the cheese rounds, so just slice the cheese accordingly and place the rounds on opposite sides of the baking dish.

HALLOUMI TWO WAYS
COURTESY BALLARD FAMILY DAIRY & CHEESE

*Ballard Family Dairy and Cheese makes Idaho Golden Greek, a halloumi-style cheese.
The Ballards use Golden Greek in a variety of ways at home—here are two of them.*

STEVE BALLARD'S POWER BREAKFAST

4 oz fresh Golden Greek Halloumi, cut into cubes
 seasonal fruit (oranges are a great addition in the winter
 months)
2 tbsp honey, or more to taste

For a quick breakfast, combine halloumi and fruit in a bowl, drizzle honey on top and serve.

TRAVIS BALLARD'S FRIED EGG AND HALLOUMI SANDWICH

 garlic and onion, sautéed
 Golden Greek Halloumi, grilled
1 egg, fried
½ avocado, sliced
 bread of your choice

Sauté or grill garlic and onions and set aside. Grill a sandwich-size piece of halloumi, or 3–4 slices, on the barbecue or in a frying pan, until golden brown and sizzling. Combine ingredients between two pieces of bread and serve.

FOSTER & DOBBS STELLAR SANDWICH

COURTESY LUAN SCHOOLER, FOSTER & DOBBS IN PORTLAND

The richness of the soft-ripened cheese combines beautifully with the sweet-hot flavors of mustard and curry pickle in this favorite Portland sandwich.

a good quality baguette
sweet hot mustard of your choice
mixed greens or arugula
3–5 slices rich soft-ripened cheese (Mt. Townsend Cirrus or Ancient Heritage Adelle would work well here)
3–4 Ricks Picks GT1000s green tomato pickles, chopped

Slice a 5- or 6-inch portion of baguette, then halve it. Spread mustard on one side, then add greens, then the cheese on top. Overlap cheese slices if necessary to create a hearty portion. Add pickles on top to taste.

Makes one sandwich.

CURRY BEER CHEESE SOUP

Artisan cheese and craft beer come together and go for a ride in this hearty soup.

2 leeks, washed
1 medium carrot
2 tbsp garlic
2 tbsp butter
1½ tsp salt
¼ tsp pepper
⅓ cup flour
2 cups chicken or vegetable broth
1 cup Rogue Dead Guy Ale
2 cups milk
¾ lb sharp artisan farmstead cheddar or aged gouda
2–4 teaspoons hot curry powder

In a large pot or dutch oven, sauté leeks, carrots, and garlic in butter over medium heat until leeks are wilted, about 5 minutes. Add salt and pepper.

Whisk flour into vegetable mixture and cook about 1 minute. Add broth, milk, and beer, gently whisking as you add. Let simmer 5 minutes. The soup will gradually become thicker as it simmers.

Add cheese by small handfuls and whisk each time to make sure each handful is evenly incorporated. Once you've added all the cheese, simmer over medium heat for about 5 minutes. Add curry powder as desired; less delivers a subtle undertone, add more for a more pronounced curry flavor.

Serves 4.

SMOKED SALMON SCALLOPED POTATOES
COURTESY SAUNDERS CHEESE MARKET, SPOKANE, WASHINGTON

- 4 tbsp butter, melted
- 4 medium potatoes, thinly sliced
- 1 onion, minced
- 1 lb smoked salmon
- ½ lb Mt. Townsend Creamery Trailhead, grated
  salt and pepper
- 1 cup heavy cream
- 1 tbsp fresh dill

Preheat oven to 350°F. Butter a casserole or gratin dish. Place a layer of potatoes on the bottom of the baking dish, sprinkle with half of the onions then layer half of the salmon followed by ¼ of the cheese. Save half of the cheese to put on top of the dish. Repeat layering until all ingredients are used. Season with salt and pepper. Pour the cream over the top, add the final layer of cheese. Cover and bake for 1 hour or until the top is golden brown. Remove from oven and sprinkle with fresh dill. Let the dish stand for 10–15 minutes before serving.

Serves 4.

SALADS

Green Salad with Pork Croutons, Pecans, and Rogue Creamery Smokey Blue

Courtesy Matthew Amster-Burton, rootsandgrubs.com

- 4 boneless pork top loin chops, ½-inch thick (about 3 ounces each)
- 2 eggs
- 1 tbsp vegetable oil
- ½ cup flour
- 1 cup panko
- ½ cup lard or peanut oil for pan-frying
- ⅓ cup extra virgin olive oil
- 1½ tbsp sherry vinegar
- salt and pepper
- 10 ounces salad greens
- 4 ounces coarsely chopped pecans
- 4 ounces crumbled Rogue Creamery Smokey Blue Cheese

Place the pork chops between two sheets of plastic wrap and pound slightly thinner. Beat the eggs and vegetable oil together in a pie or cake pan. Place the flour and panko in 2 additional pie pans. Bread the pork by dipping it (on both sides) in the flour, the egg mixture, then panko. Gently shake off any excess panko and place on a rack to dry for at least 5 minutes.

Heat the lard or peanut oil in a large skillet over medium-high until shimmering, but not smoking. Add the breaded pork chops and cook until golden brown, about 2 minutes per side. Drain on paper towels and cut into ¾-inch squares.

Whisk together the olive oil and sherry vinegar, then add salt and pepper to taste. Dress the salad greens and divide into four large bowls. Top each bowl with ¼ of the pork, pecans, and cheese.

Serves 4.

ROASTED MUSHROOM SALAD WITH SHAVED CHEESE AND LEMON-CHIVE VINAIGRETTE

COURTESY LAURA BYRNE RUSSELL

- 1 pound cremini mushrooms, quartered
- 4 tbsp olive oil, divided
- 1 tsp salt, divided
- 1 clove garlic, minced
- 1 tsp mustard
  grated zest of one lemon
- 2 tbsp lemon juice
- 3 tablespoons canola oil
- ¼ tsp fresh-ground black pepper
- ⅓ cup chopped fresh chives
- ½ pound mixed salad greens (about 4 quarts loosely packed)
- 1 4-ounce piece firm washed-rind cheese, such as Estrella Valentina, shaved into thin strips with a vegetable peeler*

Heat the oven to 400°F. Put the mushrooms on a baking sheet and toss them with 1 tablespoon of the olive oil, ½ teaspoon of the salt, and the garlic. Roast the mushrooms until they are well browned, stirring occasionally, about 20 minutes. Remove from the oven and let the mushrooms cool for 5 minutes.

While the mushrooms are cooking, make the vinaigrette. In a small bowl, stir together the mustard, lemon zest, and lemon juice. Whisk in the remaining 3 tablespoons olive oil and the canola oil to form a thick dressing. Stir in the remaining ½ teaspoon salt, the black pepper, and the chives.

Put the greens in a large serving bowl. Toss the greens with the roasted mushrooms, half of the cheese shavings, and the vinaigrette. Divide the salad onto plates and serve topped with the remaining cheese.

Serves 4–6.

* The cheese will be easier to work with if you put it in the freezer for 10–15 minutes to firm it up.

WATERMELON, ARUGULA, AND FETA SALAD

RECIPE COURTESY SAUDERS CHEESE MARKET, SPOKANE, WASHINGTON

- 3 tbsp lemon juice, freshly squeezed
- 1 tbsp Dijon mustard
-   kosher salt
-   black pepper
- ¼ cup plus 2 tbsp extra virgin olive oil
- 4 cups (about 2 oz) loosely packed arugula, tough stems removed, well washed in several changes of cold water, and spun dry
- 3 lbs seedless watermelon, rind removed, cut into 1-inch cubes
- ½ cup Whitestone Feta from Larkhaven Farm or other artisan feta, crumbled

In a large mixing bowl add lemon juice, mustard, salt, and pepper. Drizzle in olive oil. Whisk until emulsified. Add arugula and watermelon and toss. Top with feta and serve.

Serves 4–6.

CAPRESE SALAD

COURTESY JOE CHAPUT—LES AMIS DU FROMAGE, VANCOUVER, BC

A summer staple in our house, we prefer a slight twist on the traditional recipe by adding some shallots and lemon juice. If available, slices of perfectly ripe avocado also are a welcome addition to this salad. You can make a large platter, or you can make individual plates of this salad.

- 1 or 2 ripe tomatoes, preferably heirloom (choose different color tomatoes if you have the option)
- 1 Natural Pastures mozzarella di bufala (made from Fairburn Farm's water buffalo milk)
- 1 shallot
- 1–2 tbsp of small sized capers, preferably non-pareilles
- 5 large basil leaves
- Juice of ½ lemon
- ⅓ cup extra virgin olive oil. Note: We prefer l'Oulibo from Provence or Coltibuono
- Maldon sea salt
- Freshly ground black pepper. Note: We prefer telicherry peppercorns

Wash tomatoes, remove core, and slice them ¼- to ½-inch thick. Drain the buffalo mozzarella, pat it dry, and slice it the same as the tomatoes. (Note: An egg slicer cuts the mozzarella very evenly.) In a circular design around the plate, alternate the tomato and cheese slices, overlapping one another. If you have a couple of slices extra, place those in the center of the circle. Peel the shallot, remove the core and slice it very thinly. Spread the slices evenly over the tomatoes and cheese. Sprinkle the capers over the salad. Stack the basil leaves and gently roll them tight like a cigar. Slice them very thinly with a sharp knife. Sprinkle the basil over the salad. Drizzle the lemon juice and olive oil over the salad. Season the to taste with salt and pepper, and serve immediately.

Serves 2–4.

SERVING NOTE: If you are trying to prepare part of the meal ahead, you may assemble the salad ahead of time (up to 4 hours). When it is time to serve, just add the oil, lemon juice, salt, and pepper.

MAINS

ZUCCHINI GRATIN WITH BEECHER'S FLAGSHIP CHEESE
COURTESY RENEE ERICKSON, BOAT STREET CAFÉ, SEATTLE

- 1 pound zucchini (about 4 medium), ends trimmed
- 1½ tsp kosher salt, divided
- pepper to taste
- pinch nutmeg, freshly grated
- 2 tbsp fresh tarragon leaves, roughly chopped
- ½ cup heavy cream
- 4 ounces Beecher's Flagship cheese, shredded

Preheat oven to 400°F. Grate the zucchini with the grating disk of a food processor (preferred) or a box grater. Toss with 1 teaspoon salt and set aside for at least 15 minutes.

Squeeze the zucchini between your hands over the sink to remove excess water. Blot with paper towels. Toss with remaining ½ teaspoon salt, pepper, nutmeg, and tarragon and place in an 8" x 8" baking pan.

Pour the cream over the zucchini mixture and top with the cheese. Bake 30 to 35 minutes, until well browned and bubbly. Cool 5 minutes before serving.

Serves 4.

PALAK PANEER

Several Northwest cheesemakers include paneer (also spelled panir) in their cheesemaking repertoire; here's a contemporary take on the Indian classic incorporating this versatile cheese.

	butter or ghee
8	oz paneer (or more to taste), chopped into small cubes
1	tbsp coriander
1	tsp tumeric
1	tsp cumin
1	tsp garam masala
½	tsp smoked paprika
	1-inch piece fresh ginger root, grated
2	lbs fresh spinach, washed, stemmed, and chopped
1	tsp salt

Heat 3 tablespoons of butter or ghee over medium heat until sizzling. Add paneer and fry, turning cubs gently with a spatula until paneer is golden brown on all sides. Remove from pan and set aside.

Toast the spices in a large sauté pan over low heat until they release their aroma, 1 or 2 minutes. Add ginger, fresh spinach leaves (add the spinach in stages if all of it won't fit into the pan at once), and salt and increase heat to medium-high. Cover and cook until all the spinach leaves are wilted, 5–7 minutes. Stir occasionally to ensure that all leaves wilt.

Once the spinach leaves are thoroughly cooked, add paneer and stir. Cover and cook over medium heat another 5 minutes. Stir well and serve with rice and naan.

Serves 4.

GRILLED SWEET ONION, THYME, AND GOUDA PIZZA

COURTESY OF DIANE MORGAN, FROM HER BOOK *GRILL EVERYDAY:*
125 FAST TRACK RECIPES FOR WEEKNIGHTS AT THE GRILL (CHRONICLE BOOKS 2008).

*I grill sweet onions, especially the Walla Walla variety, from the moment they arrive
in the market. Of course, they're great served as hunky slices on top of a grilled burger
or steak, but nothing beats grilled sweet onions scattered over a pizza crust, especially
when a white farmhouse Gouda is melted on top. Visually, this is a beautiful
white pizza, with the flecks of fresh thyme giving it a pop of color.*

1 (16- to 18-ounce) package fresh or frozen pizza dough
1 large Walla Walla or other sweet onion, cut crosswise
   into ¼-inch-thick slices
   extra-virgin olive oil
   vegetable-oil cooking spray
1 tbsp fresh thyme leaves
   freshly ground pepper
6 ounces farmstead Gouda, thinly sliced
   all-purpose flour, for dusting

If using fresh dough, remove it from the refrigerator 30 minutes before you roll it out. If
using frozen dough, transfer it to the refrigerator a day before you plan to make pizza, so it
can thaw slowly, and then let it sit at room temperature for 30 minutes before you roll it
out.

Prepare a hot fire in a charcoal grill or preheat a gas grill on high. If the grill has a built-in
thermometer, it should register between 500°F and 600°F. Have ready a 14-inch, nonperfo-
rated pizza pan, preferably an inexpensive aluminum one.

While the grill is heating, arrange the onion slices in a single layer on a large, rimmed
baking sheet and brush the slices on both sides with olive oil. Set aside.

Oil the grill grate. Place the onions directly over the hot fire and grill, turning once, until grill
marks appear on both sides and the onions are crisp-tender when pierced with a knife,
about 4 minutes per side. (Use a combination of tongs and a long-handled spatula to turn
the onion slices so they stay intact.) Set aside.

Coat the pizza pan with vegetable oil spray. Remove the dough from the plastic bag and place on a lightly floured work surface. Lightly dust the dough with flour. Using a rolling pin, roll the dough into a 10-inch round without rolling over the edges. Lift the dough occasionally to make sure it isn't sticking to the work surface. Shake the excess flour from the dough. Lay the dough on the prepared pizza pan and gently stretch it into a 14-inch round.

TO TOP THE PIZZA: Brush olive oil over the crust, leaving a 1-inch border. Separate the onion slices into rings and arrange evenly over the pizza dough. Scatter the thyme over the top and season with a few grinds of pepper. Evenly distribute the cheese over the onions.

Place the pizza in the center of the grill directly over the hot fire and cover. (Work quickly so the grill temperature doesn't drop too much.) Grill the pizza until the crust is crisp and golden brown and the cheese is bubbly and melted, about 10 minutes.

Using a pizza peel or thick oven mitts, remove the pizza from the grill. Slice the pizza into wedges and serve immediately.

Makes one 14-inch pizza; serves 4 to 6.

DESSERTS/SWEETS

ROASTED PEACHES WITH CHÈVRE
COURTESY LAURA BYRNE RUSSELL

    3 tbsp sliced almonds
    4 peaches, halved and pitted*
    8 tbsp fresh chèvre, such as Rivers Edge
    2 tsp honey
 1½ tsp fresh thyme

Heat the oven to 400°F. Put the almonds in a small baking dish. Toast them in the oven, stirring occasionally, until light brown, about 15 minutes.

Put the peaches in a baking dish, skin-side down, and cook until tender, 20 to 25 minutes. (You can cook the almonds and peaches at the same time.) Remove the peaches from the oven and let them cool just slightly, about 5 minutes.

Spoon 1 tablespoon of the goat cheese into the center of each peach half. Drizzle each peach with some of the honey and then sprinkle the thyme and toasted almonds over the top. Serve warm.

Serves 4.

* The peaches will be much easier to halve and pit if you use a freestone variety.

BLUEBERRY FROMAGE BLANC PARFAIT

*Refreshing without being too sweet, these petit parfaits are a perfect way
to enjoy fresh artisan cheese on a warm summer afternoon during berry season.*

8 oz artisan fromage blanc
1 tsp lemon zest
2 tsp honey, or more to taste
½ pint fresh blueberries

Mix together fromage blanc, lemon zest, and honey in a small bowl. Taste for desired sweetness, as fromage blancs will vary in flavor. Aim for a subtle sweetness that balances the tanginess of the cheese without overpowering it.

In two 6-oz juice glasses, layer fromage blanc, then blueberries, then more fromage blanc and more blueberries. Top with a dollop of fromage blanc. May be refrigerated before serving.

Makes 2 small parfaits

CHEESE PLATES AND ACCOMPANIMENTS

A NORTHWEST CHEESE COURSE

Courtesy Steve Jones, Cheesemonger at Steve's Cheese in Portland

NORTHWEST CHEESE COURSE #1

Pholia Farm Hillis Peak
Ancient Heritage Valentine
Black Sheep Creamery Mopsy's Best
Estrella Family Creamery Guapier
Rogue Creamery Rogue River Blue
Pair with: Toasted Oregon walnuts and sour cherries

NORTHWEST CHEESE COURSE #2—AN ALL GOAT PLATE

Rivers Edge Chèvre Sunset Bay
Rollingstone Chèvre Bleu Agé
Fraga Farm Rio Santiam
Tumalo Farms Pondhopper
Sally Jackson Leaf Wrapped Goat Cheese
Pair with: Toasted Oregon hazelnuts and honey

Six Simple Things to Do with Local Artisan Cheese
Courtesy Connie Rizzo, Cheesemonger
at DeLaurenti Specialty Food & Wine in Seattle.

1. Mom's favorite apple pie recipe served with slices of **Mt. Townsend Trailhead.** Alternatively, lay slices of the cheese on top of the apples before the top crust is put on, then bake.

2. Fresh figs sliced in half, a goodly portion of **Rogue River Blue** on top, with a sprinkle of toasted crumbled hazelnuts.

3. Fresh crabapple paste (made by a DeLaurenti employee, Tamar) spread on thin slices of toasted Macrina Volkhorn bread topped with a slice of **Sea Breeze Farm Vache de Vashon.**

4. Port Madison Farm Fresh Chèvre rolled in crushed pink peppercorns served with fresh ripe chopped apricots.

5. Fresh Bing cherries, chopped and mixed with Lime Pickle Chutney (making it a Northwest chutney) served alongside **WSU Cougar Gold.**

6. A classic combination: **Juniper Grove Farm buche log** sliced into ¼-inch discs lightly coated with fine bread crumbs that have been mixed with crushed green peppercorns. Lightly sautée and place on top of a mixed green salad that's been tossed with a light lemon and olive oil dressing.

TWO BRITISH COLUMBIA CHEESE COURSES
Goat's Pride Tomme de Chèvre
Carmelis Goat Gruyere
Gort's Extra Aged Gouda
The Farm House Cheddar
Poplar Grove Tiger Blue
Pair with: Vij's Date/Tamarind Chutney

AN ALL-ISLAND COURSE

Little Qualicum Island Bries
Natural Pastures Boerenkaas
Hilary's St. Denis
Salt Spring Island Cheese Company Montaña
Moonstruck Beddis Blue
Pair with: Pears and toasted Vancouver Island Hazelnuts

CHUTNEY MADE EASY
COURTESY CHRISTINE HYATT OF CHEESE-CHICK.COM

SPICED CHERRY CHUTNEY

This easy, tangy-sweet accompaniment is bursting with fruit flavor and a hint of spice. Makes a great pairing with sheep's milk or blue cheese.

- 2 tbsp butter
- ½ cup onion, finely minced
- ¾ cup dried tart cherries, coarsely chopped
- 2 tbsp balsamic vinegar
- 1 tbsp water
- 1 tbsp brown sugar
- ¼ tsp ground nutmeg
- ¼ cup toasted walnuts, chopped

In a large skillet over medium-high heat, melt butter. Add onion and sauté onion until translucent, about 3 minutes.

Add cherries and stir thoroughly until coated with butter. Add balsamic, water, brown sugar, and nutmeg. Continue to cook and stir until almost all of the liquid has evaporated, about 2 minutes.

Remove from heat and add the toasted walnuts. Transfer to serving dish and allow to cool before serving. May be made ahead. Refrigerate leftovers and use within 5 days.

APRICOT AND PISTACHIO CHUTNEY

A colorful and delicious pairing for soft and mild cheeses like Havarti and Camembert, this sweet and salty chutney gets a dash of complexity from bourbon.

- 1 **tbsp butter**
- 1 **cup dried apricots, coarsely chopped**
- 2 **tsp honey**
- ¼ **tsp cinnamon**
- ⅛ **tsp salt (omit if using salted pistachios)**
- 2 **tbsp bourbon whiskey**
- ⅓ **cup pistachios, chopped**

In a large skillet, heat butter over medium high heat. Add apricots and stir until coated with butter. Add honey, cinnamon, and salt. Sauté for 1 minute, stirring constantly. Add bourbon and pistachios. Continue stirring for up to 2 minutes until bourbon evaporates. Remove from heat and cool slightly.

TO SERVE: Press chutney into an attractively shaped 1 cup measure and invert onto plate. The chutney will retain the shape and can be easily sliced with a knife.

NORTHWEST CHEESEMAKERS LISTED BY MILK SOURCE

Cow's Milk

OREGON
Ancient Heritage Dairy
Jacobs Creamery
Ochoa Cheese Factory
Oregon Gourmet Cheeses
Rogue Creamery
Tillamook County Creamery Association
Willamette Valley Cheese Company

WASHINGTON
Appel Farms
Beecher's Handmade Cheese
El Michoacano
Estrella Family Creamery
Golden Glen Creamery
Mt. Townsend Creamery
Pleasant Valley Dairy
Queseria Bendita
River Valley Ranch
Rosecrest Farm
Sally Jackson Cheeses
Samish Bay Cheese Company
Sea Breeze Farm
Silver Springs Creamery
Twin Oaks Creamery
Washington State University
Willapa Hills Farmstead Cheese Company

IDAHO
Ballard Family Dairy and Cheese
Litehouse Foods

BRITISH COLUMBIA
D Dutchmen
The Farm House Natural Cheeses
Gort's Gouda
Hilary's Cheese Company
Kootenay Alpine Cheeses
Jerseyland Organics
Little Qualicum Cheese Company
Moonstruck Organic Cheeses
Natural Pastures Cheese Company
Poplar Grove Cheese
Ridgecrest Dairy
Scardillo Cheese Company
Triple Island Farm
The Village Cheese Company

Goat's Milk

OREGON
Alsea Acre Goat Cheeses
Fern's Edge Goat Dairy
Fraga Farm
Juniper Grove Farm
New Moon Goat Dairy
Pholia Farm

Rivers Edge Chèvre
Rogue Creamery
Silver Falls Creamery
Siskiyou Crest Goat Dairy
Tumalo Farms

WASHINGTON

Blue Rose Dairy
Dee Creek Farm
Estrella Family Creamery
Gothberg Farms
Grace Harbor Farms
Larkhaven Farm
Monteillet Fromagerie
Pine Stump Farm
Port Madison Farm
Quail Croft Farmstead Goat Cheese
Quilisascut Cheese Company
River Valley Ranch
Sally Jackson Cheeses
Steamboat Island Goat Farm
Sunny Pine Farm
Twin Oaks Creamery

IDAHO

Rollingstone Chèvre

BRITISH COLUMBIA

Carmelis Goat Cheese Artisans
The Farm House Natural Cheeses
Goat's Pride Dairy at McClennan Creek
Gort's Gouda
Happy Days Goat Dairy
Hilary's Cheese Company
Salt Spring Island Cheese Company

SHEEP'S MILK

OREGON

Ancient Heritage Dairy
Willamette Valley Cheese Company

WASHINGTON

Alpine Lakes Sheep Cheeses
Black Sheep Creamery
Larkhaven Farm
Monteillet Fromagerie
Sally Jackson Cheeses
Willapa Hills Farmstead Cheese Company

BRITISH COLUMBIA

Mountain Meadow Sheep Dairy
Salt Spring Island Cheese Company

WATER BUFFALO MILK

River Valley Ranch (WA)
Natural Pastures Cheese Company (BC)

INDEX